Maugham

IVOR BROWN

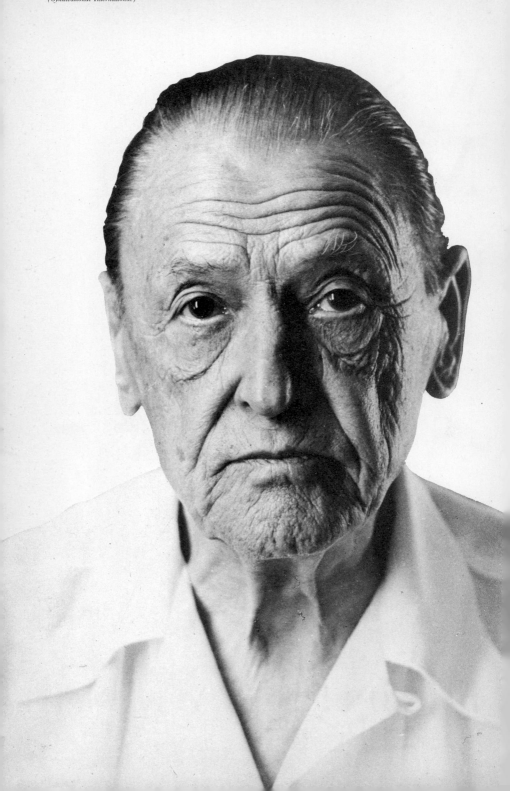

W. Somerset
Maugham

by Ivor Brown

INTERNATIONAL
PROFILES

ACKNOWLEDGMENT: The publishers wish to thank the Literary Executor and William Heinemann Ltd for permission to include extracts from *The Summing Up* and *A Writer's Notebook*.

ISBN 0 249 44005 9

Library of Congress
Catalog Number 78-104003

INTERNATIONAL PROFILES

General Editor: EDWARD STORER

English language editions published by:
International Textbook Company Limited
158 Buckingham Palace Road, London, S.W.1

A. S. Barnes & Co Inc., Cranbury, New Jersey 08512,
for sale in UNITED STATES OF AMERICA

International Textbook Company, 400 Pacific Highway, Crows Nest, NSW
for sale in AUSTRALIA

Series Design: Melvyn Gill   *Pictorial Research:* F. G. Thomas
Colour Plates: Photoprint Plates Limited, Rayleigh, Essex
Covers: George Over Limited, London and Rugby
Paper: Frank Grunfeld (Sales) Limited, London
Text: Photoprint Plates Limited, Rayleigh, Essex
Binding: Butler and Tanner Limited, London and Frome

I. The Life

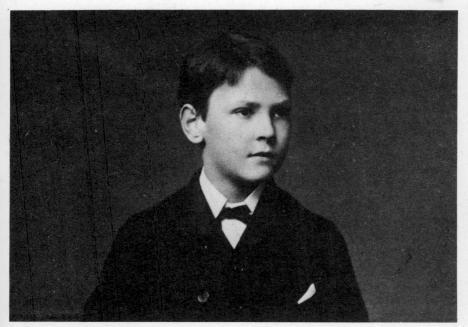

W. Somerset Maugham as a small boy (Robin Maugham)

Both the grandfather and the father of William Somerset Maugham were eminent lawyers. The family tradition was enhanced when his brother became Lord Chancellor. The grandfather founded the Incorporated Law Society and wrote many legal books. The father became solicitor to the British Embassy in Paris. There he met and married the daughter of an English army officer whose widow, having squandered a legacy, was eking out her pension by writing novels in French and composing light music. She was known for her beauty and this her daughter, Maugham's mother, inherited. Though she was consumptive she had six sons. William related that the doctors of the period thought that pregnancies were good for tuberculous patients. Their curious belief was not justified in her case. She died at thirty-eight. William, who had been born on 25 January 1874, was then only eight. His father died two years later.

As a small boy William had been to a French school and then

had an English tutor, a clergyman attached to the Embassy. He thus learned both languages in childhood: French at first was the more familiar. He remembered being told that when he was in a railway-train with his mother and looking out of the window he cried, 'Regardez, Maman, voilà un 'orse'. The orphan was put in the care of his uncle and guardian, a clergyman at Whitstable which appears as Blackstable in the novels, on the north coast of Kent, not far from Canterbury which is disguised as Tercanbury. How far is the lonely, crippled and bewildered boy represented by Philip Carey in Maugham's long novel *Of Human Bondage* published in 1915? Of this book he wrote that it was autobiographical but not an autobiography. 'Fact and fiction are inextricably mixed; the emotions are my own, but not all the incidents related as they happened.'

Since the feelings, if not the events, are stated to be authentic, the years in the cold, bleak parsonage with his austere, forbidding and self-absorbed uncle and his timid aunt, a dear creature, kindly at heart but terrified of contravening her husband's grim notions of a Christian life, must have been unhappy. The early chapters of Philip's chronicle do not give quite as repulsive a picture of Victorian clericalism and un-Christian Christianity as are to be found in Samuel Butler's *The Way of All Flesh*, but the atmosphere at Blackstable, like the house itself, is bitterly cold, deterrent, and depressing. The dominant faith with its precept that all suffering must be endured as the divine will, that every event in the Bible records an actual occurrence and that everything said about sin and damnation is the word of God, seems as chilling as an east wind in that exposed corner of south-eastern England on a February day. One shivers while one reads as Philip shivered in his icy bedroom. There is also a shiversome occasion when, having accepted his uncle's assurance that prayer can achieve anything he believes, he prays fervently to be cured of his limp and is left as lame as before. Yet, when Maugham published *A Writer's Notebook* in 1949, he quoted some sayings of his uncle jotted down in 1892. 'A parson is paid to preach, not practise.' 'Do unto others as you would they should do unto you. An excellent maxim—for others.' Evidently the Rev. Carey had a cynical sense of humour which is not presented in the story.

Philip's experiences when he was sent to the preparatory and then the senior department of the King's School at Tercanbury must be close to those of Maugham's years at the King's School of

Canterbury. Philip is handicapped by a club foot, unable to play in the school's games, and at first victimized by sneers and bullying. The author was not thus physically handicapped, but he was afflicted by a stutter with its destructive effect on self-confidence. This unfortunate stammer he had to combat in later life. The masters are mostly depicted as disappointed, ill-tempered and incompetent men, but Mr Perkins, the new Head, appears as a genuinely able scholar of humble origin. Given command in a world of snobs, he faces it bravely. He is imaginative and sympathetic. If drawn from life, he suggests at least one considerable relief at a time of boyish unhappiness and frustration. Philip has intellectual ability and is quick at his lessons. Also, as he grows up, he develops a will of his own. To the consternation both of his uncle and Mr Perkins he refuses to go to Oxford with a clergyman's career in view and decides instead to learn languages in Europe and goes to Heidelberg University.

One year in Germany was a liberation. The boy was glad to be a man of the world. The boarding-house in which he lived was crowded and conventional, but Philip met amusing incidents and made friendships. He went to the theatre and discovered with delight the New Drama of Ibsen and the Ibsenites. Also he decided that he could never be a clergyman. Maugham chose medicine on his return from his year at Heidelberg and entered St Thomas's Hospital in 1892 as a student. He qualified as a doctor after five years. Before he had finished his training he had written a novel, *Liza of Lambeth*, based on his experience of proletarian poverty, gaiety and tragedy in the mean streets of South London. It caused, he said, 'a mild sensation'. Such realism with such a background was then unexpected.

The sales of *Liza of Lambeth* were satisfactory to a beginner but not largely rewarding. But at least a small name had been made. Fortunately Maugham had come into a little money and thus could afford a year in Spain and relished it. His constant enjoyment of travel was assisted by his exceptional command of languages. As a young man he spoke and read widely in German, Italian, and Spanish as well as in the French which had come easily and naturally in his childhood. He was never the nervous tourist fumbling for a word.

He could afford to go to Paris where he pottered about the river-side bookshops and visited the studios and cafés of the talkative English and American as well as French students and artists

4

who mixed incessant argument with more occasional work at their easels. They are admirably described in the Parisian scenes in *Of Human Bondage*. He enlarged his own taste in painting by discovering the Impressionists, to whom he was introduced by the young Gerald Kelly, future President of the British Royal Academy. He found the city entrancing. In the second half of the nineteenth century France had led the world in the arts with supreme novelists and with the canvases which now change hands at fantastic sums. On its major stages flamed the magnificence of Sarah Bernhardt in the classic and romantic drama. But the realists were there too. André Antoine, a Gas Company clerk, had in 1887 founded in a very modest way his Théâtre Libre for the production of the naturalistic plays which were then being written by the *avant-garde* dramatists in other European capitals. There were cafés where the talk went on all night. He talked, listened, and enjoyed.

Paris had a spirit, an audacity, and a liveliness which London scarcely knew. It was an urban spectacle as well as an arena of the artists and intellectuals. The streets and the parks, then of course free of surging crowds, traffic-jams, and din, had colour and animation. Maugham wrote later of the sparkle and the grace of the time. Not only the carriages of the fashionable ladies and wealthy cocottes driving in their victorias with 'spanking' horses took his eye. He was charmed too by the Luxembourg gardens where 'the *nounous* with long satin streamers to their caps were pushing prams.' There was style among the domestics as well as the employers.

Back in London he shared a cheap flat with a friend busy at the Bar which meant that he was alone and able to work steadily during the day. During the next six years he wrote several unsuccessful novels and a number of unwanted plays. A single young man who is presentable and talks well can be certain of invitations. He related that when he dined out in full evening dress with tails and a white tie he could not afford a cab and took a bus to and fro. The novels were not much liked. Of the work of that period *Mrs Craddock* was reprinted in 1938 and as a Penguin in 1967. It was written in 1900 and rejected because of supposed improprieties but accepted and published in 1902 by William Heinemann on condition that the offending portions were cut. These were restored in the later editions but it is impossible to discover now what seemed so dreadful then. It is the tale of a sensitive girl who fell hastily in love with and married a beefy farmer and miserably repented at leisure. That she had a passionate but frustrated affair with a youngster more to her taste and that she could feel no grief when her husband was killed in a hunting accident was presumably the cause of the objections originally raised.

Apart from one character, the girl's maiden aunt, a detached and witty woman with a sharp tongue, the book has few merits. In an amusing preface written for a new edition in 1955 Maugham admitted that with no hesitation. He said of himself that the author of *Mrs Craddock* had shown bad taste, describing a Georgian country house as 'a blot on the landscape'. (The scene is that of the Whitstable and Canterbury country.) Looking back to the beginning of the century he described his young self as stupidly . prejudiced and affected. A member of a shallow and pretentiously intellectual set 'he admired the works of art they admired and despised those they despised. He was not only a foolish young man; he was supercilious, cocksure, and often wrong-headed. If I met him now I should take an instant dislike to him.' That is the self-portrait, written when he was eighty-one, of the author at twenty-six. He could not have been more candid.

Another book of that period, also reissued as a Penguin in 1967, was *The Magician*. Like *Mrs Craddock* it is introduced with a prefatory and valuable 'fragment of autobiography'. Maugham had abandoned the shared flat in London and found one for himself alone in Paris for the equivalent of twenty-eight pounds a year. It was thus, he said, that he first met Arnold Bennett and Aleister Crowley. The latter he regarded as a liar and a boaster who vaunted his exploits, both physical and intellectual. But he admitted that Crowley was not altogether a fake, since he had really achieved some remarkable feats of mountaineering in the Hindu Kush with none of the equipment which now assists the conquerors of the highest peaks. Without the aid of portable oxygen he had reached the top of the second highest mountain in India. He was something of a poet. An exhibitionist, he had some gifts to exhibit. More conspicuously he became infamous for his dabbling in Satanism and practice of black magic.

He reappears, at least to some extent and with his vices inflated, in *The Magician* as the sinister, seductive, mesmeric and diabolonian Oliver Haddo. Using that as his pseudonym Crowley reviewed the book in *Vanity Fair*. Maugham did not read the notice, assuming that it would be vituperative and intolerably verbose. On reading his novel he censured it as lush and turgid in style and too full of adjectives and adverbs. For that verbal profusion he thought there was some excuse in the melodramatic subject. The admirers of Maugham's later work can be astonished that he wrote this lurid and improbable story of a human vampire. He had no reason to worry about its reception and sales since 1908 was his *annus mirabilis*. A new life was opening. He suddenly found himself the dramatist of the day with royalties beginning to pour in. The author of *The Magician* had become the maestro of epigrammatic West End comedy with managers begging for more in that kind and with the leading players eager to appear in his rapidly accumulating pieces.

Among the observations made in *A Writer's Notebook* at the beginning of 1908 is this opinion of his new estate.

Success. I don't believe it has any effect on me. For one thing I always expected it and when it came I accepted it as so natural that I didn't see anything to make a fuss about. Its only value to me is that it has freed me from financial uncertainties that were never quite absent from my thoughts. I hated poverty. I hated having to scrape and save so as to make both ends meet.

If that youthful view of inevitable renown seems arrogant it is countered by the last sentence in this paragraph written by the man to whom fortune was being so generous when he was thirty-four. That ran, 'I don't think I am so conceited as I was before'.

The word fortune in this connection is not unfair. Maugham was certain to have victories on the stage before long. He said that the way to the West End was impeded, if not barred, to new writers by the predominance of Sir Arthur Pinero, R. C. Carton, and Henry Arthur Jones. The last of these, after reading one of the early novels, had prophesied Maugham's success as a dramatist because the dialogue in his stories was skilful as well as natural. The difficulty was to penetrate the profitable theatre after he had made a start with a Sunday night production by the Stage Society of his first piece *A Man of Honour*. The leading part was played by the young Granville Barker, the new darling of the drama's intellectuals (Maugham admitted his 'coltish charm' but unkindly thought him 'to be brimming over with other people's ideas'). The members of that society were regarded by the average theatrical manager as seedy high-brows incapable of laughter and dedicated to gloom. To have pleased them and irritated the critics whom

Maugham called 'the popular hacks' was no passport to Shaftesbury Avenue, the bright lights, and the royalties.

By chance Otho Stuart, who liked Shakespeare and the drama of ideas but could not live on them, was in management at the Court Theatre. He had had a failure and needed a quick replacement. It must be something with a box office appeal. He decided that the intended successor could not be properly cast. However, he had beside him a piece by Maugham. Though he thought little of it he took it as a temporary stop-gap. So *Lady Frederick* was produced and gave the doubting impresario an immediate and remarkable success. Maugham was in Italy when the news of its acceptance came. He had no money in hand and had to buy his fares with cheques whose cashing needed persuasion. In the end he reached the theatre for the first night with his last shilling.

After that the new and suddenly talked about playwright was taken up by others who had turned him down. He was in luck with his casting. Three months later *Mrs Dot*, commissioned for the magnetic Marie Tempest, and *Jack Straw*, with the immensely popular Charles Hawtrey, were staged at the Comedy and Vaudeville theatres. Another piece of less appeal, *The Explorer*, was produced by Lewis Waller at the Lyric. A record had been made. Never before had a living dramatist had four plays running simultaneously in the centre of London. 'I had achieved what I wanted', said the author succinctly and accurately.

With this more than satisfactory stimulus there was a natural concentration on the theatre. The speed and quantity of his playwriting must seem incredible to the slow worker. In the introduction to the first volume of his *Collected Plays* (1933) he wrote:

I was blamed for my fertility, which is a merit, it appears, only in the dead, but when I look back I am astounded. I had always half a dozen plays in my head, and, when a theme presented itself to me, it divided into scenes and acts with each 'curtain' staring me in the face so that I should have no difficulty in starting a new play the day after I had finished one I was engaged on. If I did not write six plays a year it is only because it would have bored me.

More will be said of Maugham in the theatre. For a while he was wholly committed and the flow of novels ceased. The theatre, now found so easy, was far more rewarding. The writing was less and the gain far greater. There are not more than twenty thousand words in a three-act play. There are eighty thousand in a novel of moderate length.

But the urge to be a story-teller returned. Dramatic writing, which in those years had to be tightly constructed and not the loose sequence of short episodes, often accepted nowadays, imposed a discipline. This had become irksome. The novelist inside him was demanding release. Maugham found himself haunted by the memories of his past; they became so obsessive that he accepted the necessity of writing a large and personal novel. In this kind of work there would be a freedom denied by the exigencies of stagecraft. So after three years of rapid and triumphant concentration on a playwright's career he refused all further contracts and settled down for two years of unremitting work on the early life of Philip Carey which, as has been said, was only factual in part but was completely true in feeling to his own progress from boyhood to young manhood. The result was *Of Human Bondage,* the longest of his novels. Unfortunately when it appeared in 1915 the war had begun and the British public was too agitated by the military disasters and appalling casualties to be much concerned with the growing pains and griefs of Philip Carey. In Britain it seemed to be submerged by the flow of bad news but in the United States, not yet involved and mourning its dead, it was highly commended by some influential critics and found numerous readers. Its success at home came later and abundantly.

When the war broke out in August 1914 Maugham could use his medical knowledge. He went to France and Flanders with an ambulance section. He narrowly escaped death in heavily bombarded Ypres when he had just moved from a spot where a shell exploded immediately after. He faced the hideous experience of working in field-hospitals. He kept notes some of which are included in *A Writer's Notebook.* The contrast of this life with that of the wealthy and successful man about Mayfair could not have been greater. There was work to be done in a school turned into a hospital into which some hundreds of wounded were packed. 'The whole place stank of pus, no windows were open, the floors were unswept, and it was incredibly dingy and melancholy.' There were only two doctors in charge, with a couple of dressers, and 'some women from the town who knew nothing about nursing'. One thing he found agreeable. He was under orders. After the independence of well-rewarded authorship and complete freedom of movement he had to do what he was told. The conditions of his medical service were revolting but he had his unaccustomed duties and discipline. For a while at least he liked doing without question what he had to do.

In 1915 he was transferred to the Secret Service where his command of languages and his natural shrewdness were well employed. He spent a year spying on spies in Switzerland and out of this came the excellent *Ashenden* stories. Then his health broke down. He had a weak chest and had had to make many journeys across Lake Geneva in bitterly cold weather. No longer wanted for Government service he took a rest by crossing to the United States where two of his plays were being staged. Then he was free to do something which he had long desired. This was to visit the South Pacific. There in 1917 he could gather material for a novel based on the life of the artist Paul Gauguin. One result of his journey was his book called *The Moon and Sixpence*. Another and larger acquisition was his contact with an entirely different kind of life rom that of the successful author and man about the West End. As he put it briefly, 'I found a new Self'.

He met people to whom books and plays meant nothing, people who were living hard and with little money as planters, traders, and sailors. They were near to nature and their manners were often crude. While they were widely different in character they had a unifying simplicity. Their ideas and tastes were not cultural. Some of their habits were primitive. But the rough diamond has its own kind of lustre. For a man with his sharpness of eye it was fascinating to watch this diversity of types.

Here were men settled amid sea and island scenery of conspicuous beauty and not concerned at all with the romance of coral islands, strange landscapes and magical sunsets. The land in their way of life was for planting and the sea for fishing and voyaging. They had their passions and prejudices. To them hardihood was essential. The delicate sensibilities of the art-loving intellectual, so familiar to Maugham, were no longer to be met. He had, as was said, welcomed war-time discipline as a contrast to his old liberty. Here was another change which proved not only agreeable but immensely stimulating.

Among his new acquaintances, so remote from the bookish people whom he had intimately known, he found matter for several books and especially for his short stories. In his collections of these there is a motley of South Sea Islanders, workers and loafers, the isolated British managers of rubber-growing estates in Malaya and

Borneo and their lonely wives, the drunks and beach-combers and the missionaries who tried in vain to rescue them from their sloth and other vices. Then there was integration of the white and coloured through urgencies of sexual need while in the clubs in the few and scattered towns the white men met to play tennis and bridge, to drink whisky and to find company which could be as quarrelsome as friendly.

Few who were not in the regular forces can have had a more strangely assorted series of assignments between 1914 and 1918. While in the Pacific he had a summons in 1917 to go to Russia where an exhausted nation was staggering through defeat and revolution. In so far as a post-Czarist Government was functioning it was that of the Mensheviks (moderates) led by Kerensky. Maugham's special mission was to Masaryk and the Czech army of sixty thousand assembled in Russia. He knew the language, having taught himself to read Chekhov in the original tongue.

The purpose was to assist the diplomatic effort of the Allies to keep Russia and the Czechs in the war and defeat the Bolshevik design, instigated by Germany, to attain a quick and separate peace by surrender. Maugham soon realized that it was a hopeless venture but in *The Summing Up* he stated his belief that there could have been a chance of success if action had been taken earlier. Too late he landed at Vladivostock, crossed Siberia by train, and reached Petrograd where Kerensky was still in power of a kind. Maugham found him serious and disinterested but unimpressive; he could handle a popular audience, but he was not equipped to tackle a revolutionary situation. The desire for peace at almost any price was overwhelming. The tide of opinion was against him and he was no match for Lenin.

After the overthrow of the Mensheviks Maugham escaped to Sweden and thence was taken to England in a naval destroyer. He had been often hungry and his tuberculosis was advancing. There was a haemorrhage of the lungs and a cure had immediately to be sought. Switzerland was an obvious goal for one in his condition but it could not be easily reached by an invalid while the war was at its height. He consulted the best known specialist and was sent to a sanatorium in the North of Scotland. The complete rest and treatment were effective. In the calm and freedom thus gained his frustrated and exhausting months in chaotic Russia could be forgotten. He had peace and privacy, his books to read and his fellow-patients to observe. His mind, he said, was never more active; his imagination raced. The writer had accumulated a mass of material abroad and there was more in the hospital where he studied the quirks of his companions.

The Scottish climate and treatment had brought such a remarkable recovery that he could henceforward undertake without undue risk travel in all kinds of conditions from which even the strongest might flinch. After leaving hospital he went to China and then to many countries and islands in the Far East. Being a wealthy man he made his journeys as comfortable as money could render them. But that could not always be managed and he had to face some hardships on land and sea. In his own words he went 'in liners, tramps, and schooners, by train, by car, by chair, on foot or on horse-back. I learned very quickly when a place promised me something and there I waited till I got it.' He never ceased to look for subject-matter and usually he found it.

There were dangers as well as difficulties but he had a useful friend, Gerald Haxton, with him. Gerald had been invaluable in making contacts with people of all kinds in the eastern plantations and in the clubs of the settlers. Maugham was shy, still hampered by his stammer, and not an easy mixer. Gerald got on with everybody and brought him the news of the friendships, quarrels, intrigues, and tragedies of life in Malaya, Borneo, and the islands, so valuable for the short stories. On one occasion the pair shared an almost fatal journey. They just missed drowning when escape seemed a remote chance and even impossible. The kind of tidal wave called a bore surged up while they were travelling by water on the Sarawak river. It submerged their boat, its passengers and its crew. They had to swim for the shore in a seething flood of water and only just reached it.

A Writer's Notebook indicates in its occasional descriptions and observations the vast extent of his subsequent movements. There were few places of interest in the Far East which he did not visit and fortunately he was physically fit and could take the strain of constant journeys in varying climates and conditions. In 1938 he was in India, meeting all classes from Princes to Yogi. For his European base he had a house in southern France and he was there during the collapse in 1940. He was shocked by the stupidity and vanity of a French officer who said that his nation had been defeated by the German 'imbéciles'. Was it a lunatic folly, he wondered, to study new methods of warfare and prepare the necessary armament? The French he found still arrogant amid

disaster. It was hopeless in his opinion to expect them to learn humility; what they might and should acquire was common-sense. When the South of France was overrun he managed to reach Bordeaux and got to America on a crowded ship. There he wrote the most brilliant of his novels, *The Razor's Edge*, with its memorable portrait of a young American who could have married well and entered a prosperous business but had an irresistible craving to find the secret of life by wandering and meditation in self-chosen poverty.

When Maugham got back to England he found the spirit of the people greatly changed. The gaiety and friendliness of the poor whom he had known intimately in his Lambeth days had been replaced, in his opinion, by sourness and envy. The proletariat was becoming a petty bourgeoisie. The old brash and beery jollity of the piano-organ and dancing in the street and of the summer 'outing' in Epping Forest, so well described in *Liza of Lambeth*, had gone. Instead there were radio and a piano in the home. Regular visits to the cinema had replaced the occasional jaunt to the South London music-halls where the most popular stars used to appear. There was the apparatus of pleasure but much less real enjoyment. He recorded the remark of a charwoman whom he had known for forty years. 'They've cleaned up the slums and the dirt and all the happiness has gone with it!' (That was partly inaccurate. There are still hosts of abominably housed Londoners. There is still squalor.) There was new and fidgety unrest despite the higher wages and absence of unemployment. The Welfare State did not guarantee well-being or contentment. Maugham did not like this new London. He was once more ready to fly from it. The last words of *A Writer's Notebook*, compiled over many years and published in 1949, are 'I am on the wing'. He was then seventy-five.

He settled in the South of France for the last years of a long life which continued beyond expectation and finally beyond desire. He had a magnificent house and grounds, the Villa Mauresque at Cap Ferrat. The burden of British taxation was avoided. He had the blue skies of the Riviera and the blue sea before him. He had a large staff and an excellent, tactful, accommodating secretary and companion in Alan Searle, the successor to the sometimes turbulent Gerald Haxton who had died in New York in 1944. He needed to have things arranged for him and they were.

He had fame, wealth, and all things handsome about him, his

W. Somerset Maugham in the early 1950's in the garden of the Villa Mauresque *(Syndication International)*

Impressionist pictures so shrewdly chosen, and his exquisite furniture. He had said that money is the sixth sense which enables man to use the others to his satisfaction. He had bought with sagacity what he liked with discretion. But with age came its infirmities which were so severe as to be afflictions. Hearing and eyesight partially failed. Deafness was a particular scourge to one who had so enjoyed conversation. He became gloomy and irascible. But the wit flashed amid the clouds. Robin Maugham, his nephew, in his book *Somerset and All the Maughams* recorded one of his last remarks. '"Dying," Willie said to me, "is a very dull dreary affair. And my advice to you is to have nothing to do with it."' Death came on 16 December 1965. He was nearly ninety-two.

Playing patience; Maugham's passion when a foursome for bridge was not obtainable

(Syndication International)

II. The Writer

Since he was born in 1874 Maugham could be counted a Mid-Victorian. English fiction was then in a transitional stage. The sovereign position of Dickens and Thackeray was a thing of the recent past. Trollope, still continuing, had done his best known work. Two who were to be accepted masters in the last quarter of the century were just arriving. George Meredith, whose early novels attracted only a small public, was reaching high regard and much larger sales. *The Egoist* (1879) and *Diana of the Crossways* (1885) appeared in Maugham's boyhood. Thomas Hardy had won attention just before Meredith. He had come into notice with *Far From the Madding Crowd* in 1874 and his reputation was further and firmly enhanced by *The Return of the Native* in 1878. In the latter book his initial description of the wild Egdon Heath had established him as a master of landscape in prose, as well as of rural character in the persons of the story.

In *The Summing Up*, published in 1938, Maugham recorded, at

17

the age of sixty-four, the various stages of his apprenticeship to letters. In it he said, 'When I was young George Meredith and Thomas Hardy seemed certain of revival. They have ceased to mean very much to the young of today. From time to time they will doubtless find a critic in search of a subject to write an article which may cause readers here and there to get one or other of their books out of a library.' The forecast was wrong about Hardy, but it has turned out to be less mistaken about Meredith. When his work went out of copyright in 1959 there was no reprinting of his novels by publishers who thought that freedom from royalties was giving them a profitable opportunity. There has so far been no revival but one never knows about the vagaries of literary fashion. In my youth I was made to understand that not to enjoy and admire, even revere, Meredith was to be a barbarian. But to Maugham this kind of writing was 'tiresome acrobatics'. In strong contrast with Meredith's show of cleverness the natural strength, simplicity, and integrity of Hardy's writing has still its compulsive power.

Maugham's first formative period came in the eighteen-eighties and nineties. Highly decorated prose was in fashion and at first he followed the vogue. He read Oscar Wilde with delight, especially *Intentions* and *The Picture of Dorian Grey*; he was 'intoxicated' by the rich pattern of words in *Salome*. One result of this pleasure was a visit to the British Museum where he jotted down the names of curious jewels and noted the titles of sumptuous Byzantine styles in decoration and exotic textiles. It was an exercise which he later regarded as absurd. His recordings, he said, were never used and are 'lying in an old note-book for anyone who has a mind to write nonsense'.

Among the exemplars in critical writing most approved by those whom Arnold Bennett called the literary mandarins were Ruskin and Walter Pater. Ruskin Maugham could only briefly admire; the verbal grandeur and the rolling sentences he found cloying when taken as a full meal. So also did Pater provide a surfeit of elegance. 'Behind those elaborate, gracious periods I was conscious of a tired, wan personality.' He admired for a while the magnificence of the seventeenth-century prose as especially shown in the surging eloquence of Sir Thomas Browne's *Urn Burial*, but he resolved that here was a flood in which he did not wish his style to be submerged. But before he abandoned the use of verbal decoration there had been one attempt in the flowery manner.

That was a travel-book about Andalusia called *The Land of the Blessed Virgin*, which after a much later re-reading he dismissed as allusive, elaborate, and boring. He found revision of a work which he so much disliked to be impossible. He felt that the book had been written by someone whom he had completely forgotten and did not care to remember. That phase of the nineties was put behind him by the young medical student and doctor at St. Thomas's Hospital among the poor of South London. It was impossible to find romance in the slums whose grey colours did not ask for the prose of purple patchwork.

At the beginning of this century the decorated style of writing was still being practised by Max Beerbohm who declared that his highest ambition was to be no more than a *'petit maître'*. Some publishers' catalogues then contained a section named 'Belles Lettres' and there was still scope for writers known as 'belletrists' in the middle pages of the weekly reviews. Max had succeeded Bernard Shaw as dramatic critic of the *Saturday Review* in 1896 and continued to hold that chair for a dozen years. He wrote charmingly round the plays of the period instead of cutting into them with a drastic surgical operation in the Shavian manner. He contributed essays in which he could be charged with gongorism. This literary habit, named after a Spanish poet, Gongora y Argote, is defined as 'an affected and pedantic style of writing characterized by the abuse of Latinisms, accumulations of metaphors, and extravagant neologisms'. Some of the Elizabethans, especially John Lyly, had gongorized. 'Max,' while the mannered style of the eighteen-nineties was still prevalent, laid on Latinisms with delight in the rare word and remote allusion. He described jockeys racing on the turf as 'homuncules scudding o'er the vert'. In an essay on 'The Pervasion of Rouge' he piled up rare words while discussing the elements and effects of feminine make-up. The ladies were said to 'ensorcel their eyes with a vermeil tinct' after they had 'farded their faces'. Maugham had, as we saw, his gongorist mood when he was a word collector at the British Museum, but he soon rejected with disdain the cult of verbal curios and 'Max' himself repented of his early fancy for the odd corners of the dictionary. The fashion changed completely. The titivated 'belles lettres' had begun to seem absurd.

Rudyard Kipling had already set a model of short-story composition. As Beetle of *Stalky and Co.* he knew his classics but as a journalist in India and at sea he knew his sailors and soldiers, his marine engineers, his Civil Servants at Simla and their contriving 'mem sahibs'. His range of English was therefore comprehensive and its use vigorous. It was not then accepted that coarse matters could be given their frankly coarse names. There could have been no possible tolerance of the four-letter words. The publishers' prim habit of refusing to print even the mildest expletives lasted for some time. But directness of statement was the new rule and gongorism had acquired the smell of a stale delicacy. Maugham developed his vocabulary when over-dressed English was beginning to seem absurd. He disliked the silks and satins of style, thought that adjectives should be sparingly used, and conveyed his meaning with economy. That was the new trend.

Typical of the old way had been H. G. Wells's engaging character, Mr Polly, the self-educating draper's assistant who got drunk on large draughts of the dictionary and was enraptured by what he called 'Rabeloosian Verboojuice' and 'Eloquent Rapsodooce'. Wells was no doubt remembering a phase of his own boyhood when he may have delighted in what he called the High Froth. But when he became a novelist he left that behind. He never frothed or gongorized. He wrote of his Cockneys and his shop-counter-hands in the language of their kind and when he moved on to write of politicians and business-men he was in command of a vivid fluency in clear communication. His narrative raced because it was not carrying the handicap of verbal overweight.

During the years when Maugham had his rush of success in the theatre and then withdrew to concentrate on the self-portraiture in *Of Human Bondage*, Hugh Walpole was becoming one of the favourite novelists with a rewarding renown which increased in the nineteen-twenties. There is no doubt that he is satirized by Maugham as the ambitious Alroy Kear in *Cakes and Ale* (1930). It is an acidly clever picture, half a justified criticism and half a cruel caricature of an author who cajoled and flattered critics, planned his social moves with the utmost care, and courted the publicity which he loved. Maugham did not deny Kear a generosity of spirit and Walpole was indeed a good friend of younger writers. This J. B. Priestley pointed out in his excellent review of authorship in his time in the autobiographical book *Margin Released*. The literary critics had been making a great fuss about Walpole; his reputation had been exalted far beyond its merits in Maugham's opinion and there is an obvious jealousy in his exposure of Alroy

Kear as a crafty exhibitor of his personality on the literary lecturer's dais, a calculating careerist and a shrewd salesman of a moderate talent.

The introductory chapter of *Cakes and Ale* in which Kear is exposed to urbane ridicule is brilliantly written. If Walpole had wished to hit back at Maugham in a novel of his own he could never have used his pen with the cutting edge of Maugham's dissecting knife. The cause of the bitterness was the opinion of the reputation-makers that Maugham was only a popular writer of magazine stories who commanded extremely high prices and was not comparable with Walpole as a man of letters. Maugham lived to see that judgment completely reversed. Walpole has now been, perhaps unfairly, forgotten. The fact that Maugham could make a fortune out of fiction is no longer held against him. Before he died his status had risen greatly and justly. He had survived the common critical folly which regards a wide popularity as a proof of second-rate work.

Another of Maugham's contemporaries, John Galsworthy, was to meet with the same injustice after the wide welcome given to *The Forsyte Saga*. Until 1920 he had had a limited but enthusiastic public among the Radicals in politics and the *avant garde* in the theatre. Therefore he was then one to whom the lofty critics could give high ranking. When the Saga had enormous sales they stupidly decided that he must be written down. Radio and television brought him back to a huge public in the nineteen-sixties. The years of neglect, and even denigration, so frequent after an approved author's death, were over. In Maugham's case the process was reversed. His rating was higher at eighty and ninety and is higher today than it was at forty and fifty.

Alroy Kear in *Cakes and Ale* is planning to write the life of Edward Driffield, an imagined author of working-class birth who had a hard struggle in youth and lived on to be acclaimed as the Grand Old Man of English fiction when he was over eighty. Because that had been the experience of Thomas Hardy Driffield has been taken as a portrait of Hardy. But the resemblance of these two is not so close as in the case of Kear and Walpole. Hardy came up from Dorset to study architecture in London at an age when Driffield was going off to sea as a poor youngster from Kent and there is no parallel in the general behaviour of the two men. But Maugham was probably thinking of Hardy when he dismissed Driffield's first work as clumsy in style and seeming to have been written with the stub of a pencil. Hardy's early Wessex novels had their awkwardness of phrase. He had yet to learn that authors of quality do not call a church an ecclesiastical edifice.

It seems curious now that Maugham attributed much of Driffield's later renown to the British habit of worshipping old age. 'Reverence for age', he wrote, 'is one of the most admirable traits of the human race and I think it may safely be stated that in no other country than ours is this trait more marked.' If Maugham had lived till 1968 he would have read of a campaign for Youth Power in British Universities and protest marches in which the academic authorities were attacked because of their age, which was never over seventy, since retirement comes in their sixties. Gerontocracy, i.e. Old Power, was stridently denounced as the curse of the nation. There are formal tributes paid to authors and artists of all kinds at their seventieth and eightieth birthdays but the salute is made to great achievement over a long period and is not the salute to senility which Maugham imagined when he was writing *Cakes and Ale* in 1930.

At that time the author most in fashion with many critics was D. H. Lawrence who died in that year at the age of forty-five. He had started writing novels at twenty-five and was soon exalted by the critics who considered themselves advanced. He was a young man writing for youth. If Lawrence had lived to be eighty there might have been none of that reverence for antiquity imagined by Maugham since his defiance of established standards of propriety would have been regarded as stale and obvious in an age accurately labelled permissive. The young were soon writing as well as behaving with a freedom astonishing to their elders. The story of *Cakes and Ale* is told in the first person and has many outbursts, irrelevant to the Driffield theme, in which Maugham was getting grievances off his chest. It is an immensely interesting book for that reason and for the same reason it is also not an example of his narrative craftsmanship. He was breaking one of his own commandments which warned the novelist against dogmatizing.

It was fatal for H. G. Wells, he thought, to be a politican himself while writing a story about politics. The really great and enduring novel cannot be a closely dated one and the novelist who stops to pronounce on issues of the time will be forgotten when 'the problem of the day' has become the problem of yesterday. It is surprising to find Maugham sniffing at *The Forsyte Saga* since, when Galsworthy came to write that remarkable portrait of a certain class in a certain age, he put behind him his early weakness of mistaking his desk for a secular pulpit. Brought up to be a solid English gentleman of the solid upper-middle class he, as a sensitive and compassionate man, had been horrified by the callousness of the London clubmen and the comfortably established land-owners who took for granted the inequity of wealth and their own immunity from hardship. In early books such as *The Island Pharisees* and *The Country House* he scolded the complacency and hypocrisy of the Edwardian gentry and their ladies. The reader feels that he is being taught a lesson.

There is severe criticism in the Saga of the Forsytes' self-centred activities and self-satisfaction in the steady acquisition of more property. But the censure is incidental to the picture of a group of people, united in their family purpose, but skilfully differentiated as individuals. The Saga brought Galsworthy far more readers than he had ever had before because it is not a sermon on the sickness of an acquisitive society, to use a Socialist phrase. Maugham should have seen why Galsworthy, who had begun as a pet of the Left Wing, became an author with an enormous public. Was there perhaps some grievance here, as in the case of Hugh Walpole?

Maugham declared that he had no illusions about his status as a writer. He said that only two important critics in his own country had troubled to take him seriously and that the bright young men who wrote essays on contemporary fiction never considered him at all. I noticed with surprise that J. B. Priestley in his massive, internationally comprehensive, and in many ways most valuable book on *Literature and Western Man* (1962) mentioned Maugham only in a single line about the Ashenden stories while Galsworthy and E. M. Forster were each given a full page, despite the latter's tiny output in a quiet, retired life lasting over eighty years.

Maugham suggested that the neglect of his work was due to the fact that he had never been a propagandist. There was, in his opinion, a prevailing taste for novels 'in which the characters delivered their views on the burning topics of the day' and that 'a bit of love-making thrown in here and there made the information they were given sufficiently palatable'. There is a thrust in that at Wells and Priestley; both made their personal opinions about the state of the world apparent when they told a story. Both have been first-rate journalists. Maugham could be called a purist in his attitude to fiction. As a novelist he would not be a publicist.

In *Cakes and Ale*, for example, he did not stop to lament the economic troubles of the nation which were indeed appalling in 1930. He did not consider it his business as a novelist to tell the Government what to do. To Bernard Shaw's belief that it is the essence of art to be didactic he was completely hostile. The story-teller or playwright who sought to instruct was straying outside his province. To provide intelligent and stimulating entertainment was the function of fiction at its best. It should present the facts of life and leave the drawing of morals to those who had a mind to be teachers. He rarely wrote about the holders of power at Westminster. When he imagined the afflicted life and sudden death of one of them in the strange and striking short story of *Lord Mountdrago* he was concerned with that exalted Foreign Secretary only as a very curious character who met a no less curious and fatal invasion of his life. His lordship's politics were incidental to his psychological obsessions and to the conflict of his personality with that of a detested opponent. The author kept his political opinions to himself.

Obviously he could have been a brilliant journalist since he had the necessary qualities of that profession. He wrote directly and concisely. He never wrapped an opinion in verbal flannel. He would not baffle the reader with a story that had no proper end and left him in a fog. That is sometimes thought to be a sign of high intelligence. To Maugham it was incompetence. This may have hampered his acceptance in the higher circles of criticism where a pretentious mistiness was taken to be evidence of deep wisdom.

He had read poetry widely and admired what he called its 'baroque' quality. He did not care for the trend begun by T. S. Eliot which made a cult of obscurity while mixing the language of ordinary speech with a dedication to mystical and religious moods and reflections. Eliot's learned allusions were not to his taste. Maugham's rationalism was bone-hard and crystal-clear. In discussing the difference between genius and talent he cited a poet of his time, A. E. Housman, as supremely talented. In making that judgment he may have been influenced by sympathy with Housman's sad, sardonic ponderings on the human condition. Maugham could not endure rhapsodies over the loving kindness of a deity who had created such a world as ours. Housman had wondered 'whatever brute or blackguard made the world'. Maugham had the same caustic view of a supposedly benevolent theocracy. But he kept that for his reflections about life and did not intrude them into his fiction.

He smiled rather sourly at the movement away from rationalism typified by H. G. Wells's sudden, but not long sustained, discovery of 'God the Invisible King' and by Shaw's faith in Creative Evolution. Among the philosophers writing in his time he preferred Bertrand Russell who had worldly wisdom, common sense, wrote good English, and was lucid, qualities not commonly found among the metaphysicians. But, when at forty, he decided to write a philosophy of his own, he found Russell's example inadequate because of his restlessness and inconsistency. Maugham abandoned his attempt to formulate a philosophic system that would be valid for him and enable him to pursue the course of his life with clearly defined principles. So he went his way without dogma, fascinated by the mysteries of human conduct and character and no longer attempting to integrate his perceptions in an all-inclusive creed.

He had matured and had finished his medical training before the vogue of psycho-analysis; the psychology of his stories was not of the kind which goes down deepest and comes up dirtiest. The mingled virtues and vices of the people whom he studied as subjects are of the traditional kinds and there is no search for motives obscurely buried. He did not accept the conventional canons of British society but he did not think it his business to censure them. The moralists and reformers had their own sphere. A novelist had his and an artist should not be a busy-body mixing ethics with the activities proper to his craft. He was justified in resenting the fuss made about the commitment of a novelist to the Left or Right in politics.

He was also suspicious of the value given to plays and books which were ill-shaped collections of psychological speculation. His tidy mind wanted clearly apparent meanings and endings which were not dodged. A. B. Walkley, the dramatic critic of *The Times* during much of Maugham's career as a playwright, once viewed with some bewilderment a German piece produced on a Sunday night by the Stage Society. It was supposed to be the last word in *modernismus*. Walkley ended his notice with this comment on its contents. 'How bad and sad and mad it was, but oh how it was psychological!' It is unlikely that Maugham could have sat through that evening. Psychology had become the modish novelty which transcendentalism had been to some Victorians. When Charles Dickens encountered in America the wise men of Boston who were entranced by this vogue he described their state of mind as 'enthoosymoosy'. It was a word of which Maugham would have approved. He had long turned against the High Froth of a recondite vocabulary and was not impressed by the even more turbid foam of Depth Psychology.

His advice to the intending author was to read a lot of the past masters and write a lot themselves. Excellence came by practice and experience. He noticed that young men and women marked for coming prominence in authorship were apt to flag after a promising and applauded start. Though he came to dislike Meredith's elaborated style he could have quoted with approval the Meredithian counsel: 'Plod on and keep the passion fresh.' He detested the view that quantity is inimical to quality and that to be prolific is a sign of carelessness and a cause of second-rate work. Too many influential critics have tended to think most highly of those who write least.

Treatises on English literature in our time, in which Maugham scarcely gets a mention, devote pages to E. M. Forster. Forster had some private means, not much but sufficient to support without constant writing one who had no taste for luxury. Had he been pressed to turn out a book a year he might have written quite frequently above his own high level. But he would have lost some critical favour by doing so. Maugham had felt acutely the need of money in his youth, and was suddenly quite rich at thirty-four. Yet he continued to work for work's sake. He felt that he could do better with more application and he did succeed in improving his powers. The greatest of novelists, most notably Dickens and Balzac, to mention only two, had been assiduous and unquenchable. It was a point, he said, for the gifted dilettantists to remember.

For most of his narrative he used a style which can fairly be called conversational. That does not mean that he was chatty. Dr Johnson, as recorded by Boswell, turned talk into literature. Maugham turned it into the kind of English that could and should be spoken by intelligent, educated men when they are describing people known and things perceived. He frequently used the first person. Evelyn Waugh attacked him for that with no good reason. To write as 'I' has its advantages, especially if the personality of the narrator has its own merits of equanimity and impartiality. Maugham was fair to all parties of a story in which there is a mixed company of likeable and unlikely characters. If Alroy Kear is mentioned as an example of unfairness he could maintain that he was unquestionably presenting a good-hearted man while satirizing a careerist.

The method allowed him to add to his own sharp observation of reality, as he saw it, an occasional and stimulating thrust of wit. A typical example of this is the wealthy American snob Eliot Templeton who figures largely in *The Razor's Edge*, a book written in the first person. This gave the narrator scope to be cutting, and rightly so, at the expense of Templeton's ridiculous obsession with titles. When he entertains, which he does with lavish generosity, he is a menu-snob with never a pause to reflect that he may be over-doing his fuss about the perfect wine for the perfect meal. His transition to the Roman Church is neatly described as a journey into the best ecclesiastical society.

At the same time there is a warm acknowledgment of the man's unfailing kindness to people who have lost their money and have never known such distress before and of the tact with which he prevents them from feeling that they are living on charity. Maugham excelled in that kind of balance and because he was writing as himself, the detached and critical friend of all parties in the book, he was able to portray them both as an intimate who had been in the same room with them and as a student of their moods who could judge them with shrewd and yet benignant discretion when he made the record reflectively and in isolation.

One notices the contrast with a much younger man who was active and prolific in the years between the two wars. That was Aldous Huxley. His friends knew him as a fertile and fascinating talker but he wrote as a writer. He relished 'verboojuice' of a classical kind and the reader who would know the exact meaning of some of his adjectives needs English, Latin, and Greek diction-aries at hand. His characters are frequently intellectuals and they do not let us forget it. They talk at length and brilliantly, radiating ideas about everything from biology to the fine arts of all ages. But one does not hear them uttering their words: they, through the author, are writing them whereas one can always listen to Maugham's voice, steady in flow, clear in delivery, never unduly excited or over-emphatic, and never puzzling with a too learned reference or a word that asks for a lexicon. In life he was the victim of a stammer, but his dialogue put to paper flows with the utmost ease. You know what he thinks as well as what his men and women think because he is there at one's elbow while the stream flows, as translucent as clear water over pebbles.

He fairly complained about the critical neglect of narrative value. I have read essays in which contemporary authors were evaluated solely in terms of psychology and characterization. It never occurred to these assessors that it is the business of the novelist to shape, sustain, and complete a plot. The hack phrase of the 'blurb' composers 'Cannot be laid down' should be completely applicable to anything really well written and especially to the story-teller's work. The best authors in this kind will not let you go until they have finished their job. Some great novelists have had many and various gifts, acute and interesting minds, a particular type of percipience, and an eye for that which the ordinary person fails to see. Impressed by a reputation one wants to read on and yet it becomes a struggle. Duty calls but the attention wavers and the mind boggles. Even those who most revere Henry James must occasionally 'get stuck'. There are others in his class who sometimes make one look forward to see how many pages lie ahead. They lack the great essential, narrative value.

In the theatre there is a thing of which Maugham was well aware. It is known as 'star quality'. It is that which seizes the members of the audience and compels them to look and listen. The play may be weak, but thanks to one or two leading players its faults cease to be noticed. This kind of personal sovereignty usually needs hard work and an expert technical equipment as well as personal magnetism, but industry and experience will not create it by themselves. Many of the most accomplished professionals lack it. They make admirable supporting players but they are not irresistible. The stars have that extra magic which is indefinable and inexplicable.

There is a similar mystery about the narrative quality in writing. Some are blessed with this compulsive power. You may not like Kipling's opinions but you have to read on. There is never any effort needed to continue. He has got you by the throat. He did not require years of application to master his craft of story-telling. In the two years after he was twenty-three he had completed *Plain Tales from the Hills, Soldiers Three* and many others of his best short stories. His brief journalistic training was a help, but in fiction he was what is called 'a natural'.

Maugham did not have that lightning start or that sudden fascinating blaze. He apprenticed himself to his life-work, studied its diversity of methods, and carefully noted the technique and even, if you insist on the word, the tricks of the supreme performers in fiction. Thus, far more slowly than Kipling but at last effectively, he became one of the 'Can't-lay-it-down' class. He was not one of 'the naturals'. Dickens, schooled like Kipling in newspaper reporting, was an immediate and inimitable novelist when he began *The Pickwick Papers* at twenty-three. Maugham had to wait and work, but he achieved his goal in early middle age. He did not dazzle as one fortunately born to be by instinct what he became by effort. But his command of narrative quality was apparent before long and beyond challenge.

III. The Playwright

The 1946 revival at the Savoy Theatre, London of Lady Frederick *(Mander & Mitchenson)*

The names of dramatist and playwright are commonly used as alternatives without distinction of meaning. Play is so inclusive a term that it drifts down from the stormy heights of tragedy through various pleasaunces of enjoyment to the bear-garden of those so hideously described as 'out for a giggle'. Drama, on the other hand, has academic and cultural status. One feels a capital D in the air. It elicits a flood of lectures and seminars. It is a subject for toiling examinees. It has now become so widely accepted as educational and as an important item of the 'Eng. Lit.' curriculum that bus-loads are driven up from the schools to attend the approved examples of this exalted subject. When the British Drama League was founded more than fifty years ago it was a pioneer in urging that the study and performance of plays by amateurs as well as professionals are a valuable public amenity and not only a personal pleasure.

When the League campaigned for national and civic theatres

and general support for this art in particular it was a lonely voice. But since 1945 its demands have been widely and lavishly met. Drama has dignity; it also has recognition. City Councillors, who would not have given it a penny of public money, are proudly endowing civic theatres at the rate-payers' expense. The theatre long suspect in Britain as Satan's workshop has the support of the Churches and the accolade of royalty for its principal practitioners. It has its Knights and Dames. It has honorary doctorates awarded by the Universities to a class of person once regarded as a wandering vagabond, scarcely acceptable in polite society, wayward, picturesque, and sometimes scandalous. The old rake has become the new teacher. If the creator of the British Drama League had wished and could have afforded to launch a big publicity drive the advertising agent could have used the slogan 'Drama is Good For You'. There is nothing it seems so uplifting as Drama.

This great promotion came during Maugham's lifetime. He said that he was never stage-struck, yet in his early youth he was busier with plays than with books. This suggests some degree of infatuation with the greasepaint world and its zest for 'Let's Pretend'. His earliest efforts to be a master of light and conventional entertainment were unacceptable to the managers in the entertainment industry. He had his first production as a newcomer in what was called the New Drama. At last obtaining a performance as a Stage Society dramatist, he was in the company of the Ibsenites and of the Radicals and Socialists in politics, Shaw, Galsworthy, Granville Barker and others whose views he did not help to promote in the theatre or anywhere else since he kept his opinions to himself. It has already been explained that his first play to be produced was presented by this group, and now he moved outward, onward, and financially upward into the theatre of normal entertainment.

Drama, with a capital D, was not congenial to him. He had had his New Drama period as a young man in Germany and France. He had seen Ibsen plain, scowling over a mug of beer and a newspaper in a Munich café. He later turned against Ibsen and included some petulant and silly criticism of that master in *The Summing Up*. 'Ibsen had a meagre power of invention; his characters under different names are dully repeated and his intrigue from play to play is little varied.' This is nonsense and invites the obvious retort that Maugham's pieces about smart society are repetitious in their persons and themes. He did not think much of Shaw's ideas, 'which consisted of no more than the common culture of the day'. Nonsense again. But he had to admit that Shaw had 'high spirits, rollicking humour, and fertility of comic invention' and that his ideas, so curiously dismissed as stale, 'were expressed with great vivacity'. In any case Maugham did not like and would not contribute to the Drama of Ideas. His thinking was on professional lines, how best to tell a story, to hold an audience, and to make dialogue effective on the stage. He did not want to be a saviour of society. He chiefly wanted to amuse and enliven it with wit that had sting and style. He would divert with comedies of modern manners those who were ready to pay for their pleasure. In 1908 he needed money, set out to make money, and to his surprise found that he soon had money.

The believers in Drama see it as a perpetual glory whose high lights never flicker and go out. Maugham would have none of that. 'The dramatist,' he said sharply, 'practises the most ephemeral of the arts'. In support of this he maintained that a play of ideas is dead when the ideas become familiar. 'Now that everyone admits the right of a woman to her own personality it is impossible to listen to *A Doll's House* without impatience.' This entirely ignores the fact that a play of ideas is not only that. It may also be a play rich in character and expert in construction which continues to compel fascinated attention. Human nature is on view while the customs and conventions of a special period are under scrutiny. The general attitude to domesticity has no doubt radically altered but there are still stupid, selfish, and possessive husbands as the reports of marital quarrels show every day of the week. Torvald Helmer who drove his wife to walk out and slam the door lives on.

It is no less obvious that, while Shaw's opinions about British society and its morals are no longer a surprise, his plays are revived with frequency and success. In fact the most discursive of his pieces which have the least action and most argument had only a tiny public when they first appeared and the ideas were fresh. Yet, with good casting, they can have a long run sixty years later. A case in point is *Getting Married* whose long and lively debate on the necessary reform of the marriage laws met with a very poor response when it was produced in 1908. But it filled a West End theatre for months in 1966. During the middle of that decade there was a 'Shaw Boom' in London, and that is quite likely to recur. The vitality of his work was not quenched by his death. Maugham wholly under-rated the potency of the serious playwright when he deemed his work to be as transient as the life of a butterfly.

The play with no ideas and much light entertainment he regarded as equally doomed. He argued that, when the social habits of the time change and a cocktail replaces a glass of sherry, there is a fatal loss of actuality. In the introduction to the first volume of his *Collected Plays* he wrote, 'With these changes a play ceases to become lifelike and becomes quaint. The spectator no longer believes in it.' In that event the spectator has a very shallow mind. The details of diet and refreshment, the vogues in dress and furnishing, are of trifling importance. The idiom and vocabulary of the dialogue may seem a trifle antiquated but what does that matter if the situations be adroitly contrived and the dialogue has sparkle? A diamond, as the jewellery advertisements say, 'is for ever'. That is true of gems of speech.

According to Maugham Oscar Wilde's plays should have perished twenty years after they were written. But along with the Shaw Boom was a Wilde Boom and in 1968 the most popular non-musical play in London was yet another revival of *The Importance of Being Earnest* at the Haymarket Theatre. Audiences are not so silly as to be worried about 'actuality'. Nobody in his senses is going to say 'rubbish' if a character in a play of the eighteen-nineties puts a message in the post which he would have telephoned in our time or asks for a brandy instead of a whisky-and-soda, a drink not yet in fashion in the eighteen-nineties.

What then of the classic English comedies which are quite often enjoyed when revived? 'The Frenchified fop of the Restoration comedy', said Maugham, 'is as dead as the heavy father of Victorian Drama.' If so, he is one of the dead who will not lie down. Congreve's rakes and dandies constantly reappear to divert us with the scandalous and stylish conversation which bedecks their routine of intrigue and seduction. In 1966 Sir Ralph Richardson appeared with his usual excellence as the heavy father in Sheridan's *The Rivals*. The old play and the animated corpse of Sir Anthony Absolute filled the Haymarket Theatre for most of a year. Old comedies, said Maugham, 'are "amusing" only in the fashionable sense of the word like wax-flowers in a glass case'. The facts have contradicted him and his contention that Shakespeare has defied the years only because of his superb poetry is curiously false. Falstaff does not live as a contributor to a Poetry Reading, nor is Hamlet immortalized only by his set speeches. The conclusion must be that Maugham wrote plays of his own kind much better than he analysed and assessed the plays of others and their power to persist.

The assertion of impermanence indicates a form of modesty. So far from seeing himself as an enduring dramatist Maugham was limiting the life of his own plays to twenty years at the most. Yet some of them have defeated his own foreboding. *The Circle*, which was produced in 1921, was revived in 1931, 1944, and 1965 in central London theatres, not to mention its frequent reappearance in repertories. *Lady Frederick*, his first 'hit' in the commercial theatre, was given a second and third chance in central London with not much result. That is understandable because it was something of an antique when it was written. Its plot, dated back to 1870, concerns the matrimonial and financial manoeuvres of the British aristocracy in Monte Carlo. There is a mixture of smart talk, which retains a somewhat tarnished glitter, with melodramatic contrivance including the 'compromising letters' and the blackmail so frequently appearing in plays of that period. Wilde, in the still revived 'society dramas' which preceded his imperishable farce, had done this before and better and he in his turn was drawing on the Parisian boulevard favourites.

Disconsolate after his experience with the New Drama Maugham was determined to achieve a sale in another and more rewarding market. He was quite frank about the method to be adopted. He would include the whole bagful of tricks likely to attract a star-actress and display her to most advantage. What sort of person, he asked himself, would both the star and the average woman in the audience wish to be? The answer was that cliché character, the titled, beautiful, charming, extravagant adventuress with a heart of gold. She must seem to have a scarlet past but is in fact more wronged than transgressing. If her first marriage was a failure, blame her brute of a husband. She will, of course, escape from her troubles of finance and re-mating because her wit is as nimble as her skill in self-extrication. Lady Frederick is all that and Irish too. And of course the other characters must be wealthy and exquisitely dressed, some by paying promptly, others by running bills. Her ladyship is a champion runner-up and can twist a claimant dress-maker round her clever little fingers.

It seemed a part made to be snapped up. But Maugham had included among his obvious gimmicks a novel incident which horrified some of the leading ladies approached. Lady Frederick generously averts the wooing of a very rich and strangely innocent young nobleman much younger than herself. To accept him would be baby-snatching as well as gold-digging. It would be easy but a

Lady Frederick, *Globe Theatre, London 1913 with Ethel Irving in the title role* (*Mander & Mitchenson*)

shame to take the money and she desperately needs to scramble out of debt. She gets rid of him by letting him see her in the morning, tousled, unpainted, unalluring. He is so naïve as to be entirely disenchanted and slips away. Apparently it never occurred to this simpleton that those who queen it in the salons of Monte Carlo at night do not look quite the same when they are woken with their morning coffee. Needless to say, there is a mature and no less opulent admirer ready to fill the matrimonial gap. Thus a play in the period style was provided with all the requisites of popularity. The 'no make-up' incident got it talked about; the dialogue had polish; the surroundings were glossy and the ending glucose. The word 'wow' was not then in use, but a 'wow' it was.

Several stars were appalled at the idea of appearing thus glamourless in the third act. One said that it was an insult to be asked to appear in such a role. (The view that leading ladies must always appear at their loveliest lasted quite a long time. Now some are sensibly willing to suit the looks to the part.) However, the player who did take the risk, Ethel Irving, backed a winner. Maugham had shown a conjuror's sleight of hand. He continued to show his expertness in theatrical 'Hey Presto'. It could be said by the believers in Drama as a noble vehicle of radical ideas and as a social benefactor that he was showing contempt for this high art. The important point is that he hated hum-bug and suspected that the High-Brows were not always guiltless of ethical and artistic fudge.

His explanation of the history of *Lady Frederick* showed his candour and his subsequent work proved his industry as well as his craft. While the plots came easily he took immense pains with his dialogue. He trimmed and cut with care. 'Cut and cut again' was his advice to the apprentice playwright. He enjoyed the use of the blue pencil as much as of the pen. 'I worked', he said, 'without the anguish of mind some writers confess to have because it was my nature.' He varied and expanded his themes; propaganda drama he could not tolerate, but from the serious and the tragic he did not shrink.

So he abandoned play-writing which he defined as the business of the young. He had worked in the theatre for more than a quarter of a century. It had been 'good while it lasted' and it had lasted long enough. Every prolific dramatist has his failures and his were comparatively few. At first his succession of swift and seemingly easy triumphs had set some of the critics against him.

Home and Beauty, *Playhouse, London 1919 with Lottie Venne, Katherine Somervell, Charles Hawtrey, Gladys Cooper, and Malcolm Cherry* (Mander & Mitchenson)

Home and Beauty, *(called* Too Many Husbands *in USA), Globe Theatre, Atlantic City USA 1919 with Ernest Lawford, Estelle Winwood, Kenneth Douglas and Marguerite St. John* (Mander & Mitchenson)

He was accused of money-grubbing with shallow flippancy and facile cynicism. Noel Coward had to live through a similar period of sneering attacks in the nineteen thirties and even one deliberate campaign to drive him out of the theatre. I remember one first night which ended in a storm of booing. Maugham had less to take. That he was not accepted as a Pillar of the British Drama did not worry him. If his plays did not last that was exactly what he had foretold. But some have not been so transient after all. At the age of fifty-nine he decided that he was out of touch with the new audiences.

He had believed, rightly or wrongly, in the importance of what he called 'actuality'. A young writer, he argued, knows instinctively what seems actual to the audience of his day because he is himself part of the social change. In the confusion of the new trends an elder man is inevitably alienated. It did not seem fitting that a senior writer should force himself into a new kind of dialogue and accommodate his usual type of plot to shifting customs and codes of behaviour. He for one could not be a senior man determined to be up to date. That he thought to be futile and pathetic. Probably he was unduly pessimistic about his own rigidity but this was the view which he reached when the tide of opinion was no longer going his way. He was not resentful but he was resigned. When, after the production of *Sheppey*, he announced his resignation he was called on for a host of interviews with the Press and explanations of his resolve. He gave the reasons just stated.

'A play without an audience', he maintained, 'is as little as colour without a spectator'. The parties to a play are usually considered to be three, actor, author, and director (once called producer). Maugham insisted on the importance of a fourth, the people who either chill a play's effect by lack of enjoyment or enhance it by the warm appreciation which makes them the fourth partners in the enterprise. He did not approve of those earnest people who form play-reading groups. 'The play that is read differs not at all from that monstrous product, once fashionable, the novel in dialogue.' He had previously felt that he had the knack of 'getting' his audience. It was not in the popular theatre in Britain receptive of abstract ideas. It was inclusive of the stock-broker and his clerk, the matinée lady whom Terence Rattigan has called Aunt Edna and the 'bright young person' who is just discovering the theatre and happily accepts its world of illusion. The various classes of play-goer have few thoughts in common, but they have the same

Our Betters, *Hudson Theatre, New York 1917 with Diantha Pattison, Fritz Williams, Joseph McManus, Crystal Herne, Rose Coghlan, Arthur Chesney, Ronald Squire, John Flood, Leonore Harris* (Mander & Mitchenson)

Our Betters, *Globe Theatre, London 1923 with Reginald Owen, Margaret Bannerman, Alfred Drayton, Constance Collier, Ronald Squire, Stewart Sage, John Stuart, Marion Terry and Alice Mosley* (Mander & Mitchenson)

feelings and a similar interest in seeing characters brought to life. To appeal to them the playwright must aim at an average capacity for enjoying a play. Maugham had long gauged the middle range of susceptibility to theatrical impact. But the emotional response on which he could rely was no longer there. He was beginning to feel out of date.

There had been at the end of his career in the theatre a sustained effort to enter new and far more difficult territory. He took for subjects the victims of life's cruelties instead of the beneficiaries of easy money, the people inclined to easy virtue and to what Mr Hugh Williams has called 'the flip side of love'. Nobody could call the author of *The Sacred Flame* (1929), *For Services Rendered* (1932) and *Sheppey* (1933) a trifler evading the most serious crises and harassing bewilderments of life. In each of these pieces suffering is the central theme and in two of them the pain is beyond remedy. The first of them had a critical reception probably beyond his hopes. Of the second he said that he expected nothing. The third had a brief run. He had thrice dramatized crippled or impoverished lives. If he had grouped his plays in the Shavian manner he could have given this trio the title of 'Plays Extremely Unpleasant'.

Lady Frederick has been described in some detail as a typical example of the Plays Pleasant, but far from Shavian, which the public wanted and which he could astutely provide in 1907. It may therefore be worth while to examine in a similar way the last stage of the playwright's progress from the gaily trivial to a new form of 'actuality', unmerited affliction by physical disaster or grinding poverty. Accusations of glib and shallow cynicism and a merely commercial motive were now wholly absurd. He had his doctor's training and a tragic family accident in mind but he was also moved by the condition of the nation.

A nephew of Somerset Maugham, Ormond, son of his brother Charles, had been crippled as a school-boy while climbing a tree and was wholly paralysed until he died at twenty-five. This terrible misfortune may have suggested the character of Maurice Tabret, an airman completely immobilized by a broken back who is found dead at the end of the first act of *The Sacred Flame*. He had been distinguished in the war and had crashed on a peace-time flight. He had been a man of high spirits and energy, most happily married. Now he is attended by Stella his young wife who sees nothing ahead of her but dedication to a sick-bed and denial of a

The Circle, *Vaudeville*, London *1931* with Allan Aynesworth, Athene Seyler, Celia Johnson and Peter Hannen (*Mander & Mitchenson*)

The Letter, *Playhouse*, London *1927* with Nigel Bruce, Gladys Cooper, James Raglan and Leslie Faber (*Mander & Mitchenson*)

complete married life. It seems that Maurice has taken an overdose of a powerful sleeping-pill. The bottle has been safely kept on a high shelf and he could not possibly reach it and so obtain more than the single tablet put normally beside him in case of need. The family doctor is going to diagnose heart-failure as the cause of death.

His nurse suddenly says that she cannot accept this and will insist on a post-mortem, appealing to the coroner if the doctor will not arrange that. She knows that the frustrated Stella has been the lover of Maurice's brother Colin and has become pregnant. The nurse, a warped and passionate woman who has been devoted to Maurice, suspects that Stella has murdered him and insists on inquiry and explanation. So the sinister story develops in a tightly written play. Stella, innocent of giving the overdose, is tortured by conscience and terrified of the exposure of her love-affair. Colin and the doctor are no less aghast since the nurse can bring some damaging facts into the open. Not apparently involved until the end is Mrs Tabret, the mother, who ends a play of taut suspense by providing the explanation.

The playwright's skill in adding shock to shock, instead of laugh to laugh, could hardly be better shown. But, though Gladys Cooper who had done brilliantly in management and personal performance in others of Maugham's plays, added to her stature as an actress in the part of Stella, this could not be a 'box-office' piece. The public did not then, nor did it afterwards, take warmly to a favourite author who was asking them to sit up and shiver instead of to sit back for comfortable entertainment. There was a further break with the Maugham tradition. There was a deliberate use of a heightened form of dialogue replacing the usual curt and conversational style. The language, he admitted, was perhaps difficult to deliver compared with his previous composition of the easily speakable line. Some critics accused him of writing a 'literary' play because of the unusual images and ample vocabulary, but literature is not a vice. The somewhat cryptic title was presumably taken from Coleridge's lines:

> All thoughts, all passions, all delights
> Whatever stirs this mortal frame,
> All are but ministers of Love
> And feed his sacred flame.

There are passions of several kinds in the play, jealousy, sensuality, and devotion. The character of the mother is one of the finest of the

Rain, *Music Box, New York 1935 with Tallulah Bankhead as Sadie Thompson*

(Mander & Mitchenson)

playwright's creation.

There was to be another devoted mother in *For Services Rendered*, again a beautiful creation. When Robin Maugham wrote of his uncle that 'With few exceptions Willie did not like the opposite sex; the only pleasant heroine in any of his books is Rosie Gann in *Cakes and Ale* he may have been right while limiting his generalization to the novels. But there are two notable and admirable heroines in these two plays. Maugham was very far from having an anti-maternal complex. He had loved and soon lost his mother and always kept her photograph beside him.

In the second of the final pieces, which can fairly be called tragedies, he put an even greater strain on an audience unprepared for a household as bleak and doom-laden as a home in Ibsen's darkest Norway. While taking an exacting and fortunately successful open-air cure for tuberculosis in the north of Scotland in 1917 Maugham, working in bed with mittens on his numbed fingers, had put together his light and almost farcical comedy about a post-war matrimonial tangle *Home and Beauty*. It was produced with excellent results in 1919 and has been several times restaged including a revival by the National Theatre Company in 1968.

There was none of this 'flip side' of war when *For Services Rendered* was written. In the middle-class family of a Kentish solicitor are his son Sydney, totally blinded in the war and condemned to a blank and barren existence, and his sister Evie who is giving her life to looking after him. She herself lost her fiancé in the war and has never recovered. She endures the attendance on her incapacitated and sometimes churlish brother, but for relief has turned her starved affections to a young naval officer who has been 'axed' from the Service and invested his little capital in a garage business for which he has no aptitude. He is caught by the economic depression of 1931 and faces not only ruin but imprisonment since he has been stupidly handing out dud cheques in the vain hope of pulling through. Finally cornered he shoots himself. If he could have remained in the Navy he would have done well, but now he is indeed a peace-victim. There is another ex-officer about the place, one who had enjoyed the war because it made him 'a temporary gentleman' in a way of life where, out of the trenches, whisky flowed and women were free and easy. Married to Evie's sister, he is a lecherous alcoholic.

When Evie loses her sailor, at whom she has been flinging herself in despair and in vain, she loses her balance and becomes

The Breadwinner, *Vaudeville, London 1930 with Jack Hawkins, Peggy Ashcroft,*
Margaret Hood and William Fox (Mander & Mitchenson)
The Breadwinner, *Arts, London 1944 with Laurence Payne, Jean Anderson, Ernest Jay,*
Sheila Burrell, Denys Blakelock and Constance Lorne (Mander & Mitchenson)

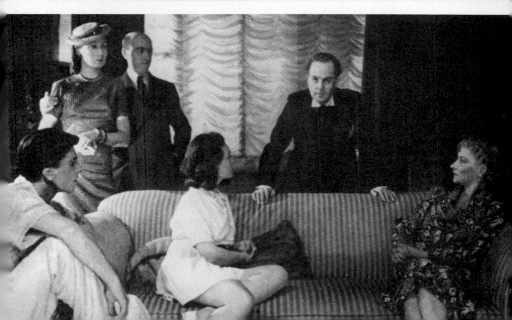

insane. The father of the family is a smug, complacent fool who cannot see what is going on. His third daughter, despairing of marriage in a world which has lost so many men, becomes the mistress of an elderly rake. The mother, a model of patience and percipience, learns without shock that she is dying of cancer. After 'Home and Beauty' had come Maugham's 'Home and Hell'.

He knew the public would not take an evening of unrelieved inferno and it did not. But he had made his protest at the callous England with its crippled or ruined tenants of 'the land fit for heroes'. He could, as he said, have mitigated the dosage of calamity, but he would not do so. There are great theatrical possibilities, especially in the role of the distraught and finally demented Evie. The author has left a tribute to the pathos and power of Flora Robson in that part. He could have hoped that a public which had so astonishingly welcomed the relentless realism of Robert Sheriff's war-play *Journey's End* would have been ready for this mordant study of war's aftermath. But perhaps the introduction of cancer, which is irrelevant to the general theme of the play, made it too hard to bear.

In Maugham's final rejection of 'escapist' theatre the central point is the unjust hardships, even extreme hunger, suffered by the victims of nation-wide unemployment in the slump years which began in 1931. *Sheppey* is a curious play somewhat reminiscent of John Galsworthy's early work. The central figure is a steady, reliable, popular barber's assistant, sure of his job. He is sensitive to the distress of the time. He draws a lucky ticket in a big sweepstake and wins what is a small fortune to him and his family. On hearing the news he has a sudden stroke, collapses, and on recovery seems to have an altered personality. He tells his wife and daughter that his eyes have been opened and that he will seek the Kingdom of Heaven by giving away all his new wealth to the victims of the poverty that is grinding the faces and pinching the bodies of the workless.

He starts by handing out money to a distressed prostitute and an incurable thief and even brings them to stay in his home. His daughter, who has seen another kind of heaven opening before her with ample money for her coming married life and then finds it snatched away by Sheppey's almost lunatic largesse, is naturally furious. His wife, although puzzled is much more tolerant, even when he brings in these preposterous guests. (We are again presented with a kindly picture of a mother.) When doctors are called

For Services Rendered, *Globe, London 1932 with Cedric Hardwicke, Diana Hamilton, Marda Vanne, Flora Robson, Marjorie Mars, Ralph Richardson, Louise Hampton, Phyllis Shand and S. J. Warmington* (Mander & Mitchenson)

Sheppey, *Wyndhams, London 1933 with Cecily Oates and Ralph Richardson* (Mander & Mitchenson)

in they pronounce him insane to the great satisfaction of the girl who has been praying 'Oh God make them call him potty!' Sheppey has an hallucination that Death is in the room with him. The vision becomes a reality. He dies quietly and the money remains in the home.

A spectre in a Maugham play? It was disconcerting and it proved deterrent to audiences. Moreover he had written better of the well-to-do folk whom he knew than of the Sheppey class of whom he knew very little. He had neglected his own advice to cut and cut again. The play limps on with an increasing lack of plausibility. It was a curious occurrence that the last character to appear in a Maugham play should be Death who, in this case, may be said to have delivered a finishing blow.

Among his novels filmed, *The Razor's Edge* was notable. Of his own short stories he took part in the scripts of one set of three, working with R. C. Sherriff and N. Langley in the case of 'Trio' (1950). A second series 'Encore' had screen adaptations by T. E. Clarke, A. Macrae and Eric Ambler. They have been much liked on television screens. *Rain,* based on one of his best short stories, was a success on the stage and even more so as a film.

But one thinks primarily of Maugham as a theatre man in London, New York and other capitals and not as a source of rich material for script-writers in Hollywood. He related his fondness for an empty auditorium while a dress rehearsal was developing; he did not enjoy his first nights. No playwright does. He was most at ease in solitude at his desk where, he said, 'you can earn most money when you work merely to please yourself. Please yourself and you are most likely to please the public.' There is no shame in that. 'It is not immediately obvious,' he added, 'why a play that people do not want to see is more artistic than one they do.' He cited the case of Bernard Shaw. Was he that despised creature, a commercial dramatist, when he wrote *Saint Joan* and a great artist when he laboriously compiled his metabiological pentateuch, *Back to Methuselah,* and scarcely ever revived even in its actable portions?

Maugham ridiculed the pretence of the intellectuals that there was a special merit in keeping a theatre empty. He did not want to banish the 'Drama of Ideas', but he maintained that in the theatre ideas and feelings should be fused in a way appealing to the average play-goer. In his last three plays there were strongly pronounced ideas about the pains and penalties of human life in

48

an unjust and agonizing world and they were given strong emotional presentation. If they failed to recapture the old success that may have been because he now excessively emphasized the suffering. He was, as he admitted losing contact with the new audience which had grown up while he was growing old. If the theatre can be called a battlefield he left it with honour for services rendered and without chagrin when he knew that it was time to go.

The Painted Veil, *MGM film 1934 with George Brent and Greta Garbo* (Mander & Mitchenson)
The Letter, *Warner Brothers film, 1940 directed by William Wyler, with Herbert Marshall, Bruce Lister, Bette Davis and James Stephenson* (Mander & Mitchenson)
My Two Husbands, *Columbia film, 1940. Loosely based on* Home and Beauty. *With Harry Davenport, Jean Arthur, Fred MacMurray, Melville Cooper and Melvyn Douglas* (Mander & Mitchenson)

Rain, *United Artists film version 1928 with Gloria Swanson as Sadie Thompson*
(Mander & Mitchenson)
Rain, *Feature Productions film, 1932 with Joan Crawford as Sadie Thompson*
(Mander & Mitchenson)
Rain, *Columbia film, 1953 with Rita Hayworth as Sadie Thompson* *(Mander & Mitchenson)*

IV. Belief and Opinion

(Cecil Beaton)

The harsh Christianity of the later Victorians was unlikely to kindle a warm faith in any young man with an active mind and broad sympathies. Instead it was a school for sceptics. In the life to which young Willie Maugham went as an orphan in the home of his uncle, the Reverend Henry Macdonald Maugham, a morose parish clergyman, there was abundance of religious observance and very little Christian charity. Church and chapel were worlds apart. The vicar would not speak to the Nonconformists in his parish. In his house he was a gloomy master. His wife had to be secretive in her acts of kindness.

The clergy of the neighbouring parishes were remembered by Maugham as contemptible. 'One of them was fined in the county court for starving his cows; another had to resign his living because he was convicted of drunkenness.' Education was clouded over by a dark and dismal creed. His schoolmasters at Canterbury were in holy orders; he found them stupid and bad-tempered. His uncle complained that he was the only man in his parish who worked seven days a week, but in fact he did very little except take the two routine services on Sunday and preach routine sermons. There was nothing to encourage a boy's interest or win his sympathy for a lively and stimulating religion.

The faith in vogue was a negative formula of prohibitions and menaces. Prayer was regarded as essential with the hope that it could be effective. Willie fervently and faithfully prayed to be relieved of his stammer which was a cruel joke to some of his loutish school-fellows and an irritation to his irascible pedagogues. The supplication to God received no answer. The faith diminished and soon disappeared. It was not surprising that he later rejected his uncle's idea that he should take up a parson's life at the conclusion of a university career. He decided that he would rather serve men through medicine, which did heal at least some of the suffering bodies, than a God, if there was one, who had made a world containing so much unmerited pain.

In some of his reflections in *The Summing Up* on what H. G. Wells called 'first and last things' Maugham wondered why there should be so much insistence on lauding the deity. He quoted an elderly and truly religious friend who read prayers to his household every morning but struck out of the Prayer Book all passages praising God. This good man argued that it was vulgar to praise people to their faces and that he could not believe that God was so ungentlemanly as to like such flattery. Maugham commented, 'At the time it seemed to me a curious eccentricity. I think now that my friend showed very good sense.' He wondered whether God knew that he was there if he had to be constantly reminded of the fact in church.

He was not crudely rejecting belief. He read widely about religious creeds and practices of the world down the ages. He could sense the appeal of Mysticism and its raptures, but that could only comfort and inspire a rare type of person. The ecstasy was valid for a few. In a long chapter in *The Razor's Edge*, which he advised readers to skip if they wanted to get on with the story, he discussed Larry's acquisition of peculiar powers of healing which are seen as effective in the story and of great benefit to the pain-racked Maturin. Maugham, like Larry, continued an unremitting search for truth. 'I have sometimes gone back beyond Mohammed, Jesus and Buddha, beyond the Greeks, Jehovah and Baal, to the Brahma of the Upanishads.' He found in that self-created and independent spirit a grandeur which satisfied the imagination. But he could discover no point of intellectual rest.

No conception of God met all the needs of reasoning man, and he remained a rationalist. This attitude was quickly reached in his youth when he was rebelling against what Shaw called Crosstianity, the demoralizing belief that our sins are wiped off the record by the agonizing death of a Saviour. To cry, 'What is it that makes me clean? Nothing but the blood of Jesus' was not a form of community singing which appealed to him. He agreed with Shaw that the evil done remains evil. If we have injured and killed, the results abide and we cannot slide out of our responsibility. What he had quickly decided in youth was confirmed by his study of the accepted philosophers and theologians as well as of the heretics. He tried to compose a system of thought about the origin and purpose of life and a code of morals which would satisfy his mind, but he abandoned the attempt.

One theory was particularly objectionable to him. This was the belief of many Christians that suffering is good for us. The idea of compensation in an after-life, 'No Cross, No Crown', seemed ugly as well as unreal, and the further notion that our characters are improved by physical distress was also insupportable. He had seen plenty of pain in his hospital years; he had watched its effect in his sanatorium months; he had been grievously ill, and in his old age he had known the failure of his faculties. The conclusion was that suffering, so far from ennobling, made for peevishness, narrowness, and selfishness.

In a passage in *A Writer's Notebook,* which he jotted down in 1917 when his tuberculosis was at its worst, he wrote:

I have suffered from poverty and the anguish of unrequited love, disappointment, disillusion, lack of opportunity and recognition, want of freedom; and I know that they made me envious and uncharitable, irritable, selfish, unjust; prosperity, success, happiness have made me a better man. The healthy man, if he can exercise all his faculties, is happy in himself and the cause of happiness in others.

He added that he had nothing but horror for the literary cultivation of suffering which has been so fashionable of late. He had no sympathy with Dostoievsky's attitude towards that. He appreciated the compelling power of the great Russian novelists, but he did not share their opinion of self-improvement through acceptance of poverty and pain. These he held to be demoralizing.

While the larger metaphysical problems were found to be

54

beyond a satisfactory solution, he had his positive ideas about the best kind of life and the ethical code which it involved. His reading in English of the Greek classics had led to his belief that Aristotle was the wisest of philosophers. So he was attracted by the idea of 'the golden mean', which the Latin poet Horace adapted as 'You will go safest in the middle'. Counsels of moderation seem dull to the romantic, the mystic and those who believe in total dedication to a cause or a creed enthusiastically held. But they make sense to level-headed people of whom Maugham was essentially one. He kept, as we say, 'both feet on the ground' and was never Willie-head-in-air. To have viewed the world through a hospital ward was a cautionary start and Lambeth had its lessons in realism. The doctrine of the golden mean in behaviour is practical in the balance which it suggests between the brain and the body, the spirit and the flesh. There are limits to the reflective as well as the physically satisfying life. The novelist and dramatist worked and thought hard while he relished the spectacle and tasted without excess the pleasures of the world. He lived according to his tenets. One might describe him as a temperate hedonist and a philosopher who enjoyed a good dinner as the companion of a good argument.

The evolutionary process has produced in man a creature with mind and senses for his use. The employment of both in fair pro-portion seems reasonable. That double exercise must depend on the retention of mental and physical health. For one who has been granted that good fortune, happiness is to be found in the mixing of sensory and mental activity. It is as foolish to be wholly intel-lectual and a Stoic as to be wholly a sensualist and an Epicurean. Maugham was neither kind of extremist. His common sense told him that happiness, which it is now fashionable to call by the Greek word euphoria, a kind of pedantry he disliked, is not a thing to be deliberately pursued. To plan for it is to lose it. It is a by-product of the freely chosen and freely practised work to which a man's natural capacities are suited.

Not all can hope for that liberality of life. Indeed far too few are so fortunate. But for those who are congenially engaged and not inhibited by repressions and distressed by failure, happiness happens. It cannot be won by contrivance. Excess in any direction leads to weariness and disillusion. Nobody knew that better than Shakespeare. When driven 'frantic-mad with ever-more unrest' by his Dark Lady, he deplored the futility of sexual indulgence, with its 'expense of spirit in a waste of shame' and with lust 'enjoyed no sooner but despised straight'. Many Elizabethans were extremists, not Aristoteleans. No middle path for them. They would be at the top or fall. They drove at their pleasures and paid for it. Their politics were a death-trap and their extravagance in foppery wanton. Recklessness and self-indulgence did, however, pay their dividends in superb poetry. The 'golden mean' invites good prose. Maugham proved the truth of that.

At the beginning of this century, the work of a French philosopher, Henri Bergson, was much read and discussed. He was breaking away from the heavy Germanic systematic thinking, which had been the fashion of the schools. He championed the *élan vital*. He proclaimed freedom from determinist theories of conditioned conduct. He had an ally in Bernard Shaw, who denounced Darwinism and preached Creative Evolution in which life could be altered and improved by will-power. Maugham did not subscribe completely to Bergsonism. But he was a vitalist in his general attitude. The poised and well-proportioned life must be enhanced by the natural vigour of those who bring energy to their enjoyments. When he wrote of the happiness to be found in action, he was not thinking only of those who work at the desk of the author or administrator. It was not, he said, a literary man's illusion that the best pattern might be that of the peasant who, with good soil in a favoured climate 'ploughs his land, reaps his crop, enjoys his toil and enjoys his leisure, loves, marries, begets children and dies'. He could have added, in consonance with his general view of life, that the peasant should be secure in the ownership of his land and able to enlarge it, at least to a moderate extent. Maugham was no Socialist or equalitarian. He foresaw a possible victory for Communism across the Western world, but he could confidently hope that he would be dead before that happened.

If the reasonableness of the balanced life be admitted then it seems logical that all should have the chance to achieve that state. Therefore the aggression and domination of the strong were morally wrong. He believed in the necessity of personal ownership and of freedom to be richer than one's neighbour; that gave stimulus to work. Release from poverty made possible lawful and admirable enjoyments hitherto denied. That had been his personal experience. But it should involve the right of all who can to prosper and surpass. The golden mean was not to be confused with mediocrity whose appropriate adjective would be leaden. He admired the excellence which emerges out of difficulty and hardship, aware that he had himself so emerged.

With the natures of truth and goodness he wrestled. There remained the mystery of beauty. In his youth he was convinced that the great work of art was:

. . . the crowning product of human activity and the final justification for all the misery, the endless toil, and the frustrated strivings of humanity. So that Michelangelo might paint certain figures on the ceiling of the Sistine Chapel, so that Shakespeare might write certain speeches and Keats his Odes, it seemed to me worth while that untold millions should have lived and suffered and died. And though I modified this extravagance later by including the beautiful life among the works of art that alone give meaning to life, it was still beauty that I valued. All these notions I have long since abandoned.

From this confession, he had once been the complete aesthete. He had breathed that very rarefied air among the café dilettantes in the eighteen-nineties. He remained an aesthete as a collector of things which he found fascinating to the eye, possessions which continued to be an agreeable addition to existence. But in a curious way he reacted strongly against beauty as an ideal. He, who had gazed and admired, decided that 'beauty is a full stop'. The enjoyment ceases and cannot be repeated. Beauty piled on beauty, he said, can become a bore. It is like a mountain peak. You climb it, are faced with a superb view and then come down again. 'Perfection is a trifle dull.' It is better not achieved. Even beauty can lift you up and let you down.

Beauty, he might have added, while pursuing this line of thought, is a holiday emotion. One comes to out of a crowded and mainly ugly town or escapes after weeks of long accustomed work in familiar and shabby surroundings. The picture gallery in a foreign city is a treasure-house. The sea and the mountains are entrancing. But how long does the rapture endure? There can be a surfeit of supreme loveliness. Scenery too can be a full stop. I myself remember some weeks of fine weather in the north west of Scotland. The wonder of the peaks that stabbed the sky, the sea-lochs winding into the glens, and the desolate moors where the air made you feel that you were being born again amid the blues and the purples of that wilderness, provided ecstasy for a couple of weeks. But I felt that perfection could pall; and that beauty was becoming a routine. The glory dwindled with the repetition of the lustrous days. I understood why people who spend all their lives as crofters, shepherds, game-keepers and fishermen in the Highlands and Hebrides hardly notice that they are living amid what to others is stupendous beauty. Maugham would have sympathized with my changing mood. He continued to savour the feast of beauty with discretion, but he felt it must be a movable feast. He once said bluntly that scenery is tedious, but he could not have felt that unless he had known it as a permanent neighbour on the Blue Coast. A balanced climate, like a balanced life, includes some rainy days. The finest poetry is not to be read nor the finest music heard in chunks. There too there is a mean.

He came to despise those whose main business is the contemplation and appreciation of art. He found that the full-time aesthetes became vain, complacent and disdainful of the ordinary folk who do the necessary work of the world. He thought these specialists and whole-time connoisseurs drug-fiends but that unhappy type of addict does not set himself on a pedestal from which to look down on his fellows. All kinds of intellectual snobbery were offensive to him. He had been its victim in the assessment of his writing during his middle period. The literary mandarins had sniffed and he liked them no more than he liked the sniffers in an art gallery or a concert hall. He said that he took it as natural that 'the world of letters should have attached no great importance to my work' because the pundits were not interested in story-telling and it was the narrative craft which fascinated him. He claimed not to be worried by the neglect, but no artist really likes to be overlooked and the aloof critics on their heights must have strengthened his contempt for those who pored over the minutiae of the arts without interest in or affection for the common life on which the artists of all kinds had to draw for their material.

From many of his plays and stories, one might conclude that Maugham was almost exclusively concerned with two widely contrasted types of character, the settlers and sailors who roughed it in the Far East, and the Mayfair rich who, perfectly tailored and costumed, moved smoothly from their elegant dinners to their sexual intrigues. On his upward path he may have appeared to be a social climber but his attitude to 'Our Betters' was as derisive as the title of that comedy implies. The fawners and flatterers he ridiculed. The intellectual snobs he detested. Moreover he did not omit the middle class from his scrutiny. He came from it. All ranks of society are seen as the prisoners 'Of Human Bondage'. The tragedy of the family solicitor's home in *For Services Rendered* might be called a middle Classic.

In his revulsion from the supercilious attitude of those once called high-brows and now more commonly known as egg-heads, he passed to the opinion, surprising to some of his readers, that beauty could be as much manifest in decent and civilized behaviour as in the creations of the brain and hands. The phrase 'gracious living' has come into fashion since his time. He looked at grace in both of its senses; it was to be found in conduct as well as in appearances. Good manners for him were a form of poise as much to be found in personal consideration and social courtesy as in the performance of a ballet at the highest level of expertise. He even went so far as to say, towards the end of *The Summing Up*: 'art, if it is to be reckoned one of the great values of life must teach man humility, tolerance, wisdom and magnanimity.'

Teach? Was he abandoning his view of the author as a detached and isolated realist who observed and recorded but should not confuse his portraiture of life with the scoldings of the social reformer? He had been averse to the 'advanced' dramatists who used the stage as a dais for doctrinaire preaching. Propaganda, he insisted, was no business of the artist. He did not altogether discard that view, but by his use of the word teach, he was admitting and even insisting on the ethical function of the arts. The good novel, it now appears, would make us better citizens with increase of understanding, sympathy, charity and the accepted virtues. He had praised Shaw's wit and vigour and regretted his propensity to be didactic. Yet if the promotion of wisdom be the office of the artist, he was sliding towards the Shavian conception of the artist as occupying a Professorial Chair of Moral Philosophy. Perhaps he was being rather careless when he let the word 'teach' slip into his last words on his profession as an author.

It is not aggravating, indeed it is almost refreshing, to find that Maugham, usually so exact in self-expression and so rational in exposition, could be sometimes open to a charge of inconsistency. When meeting the same accusation Walt Whitman had bluntly retorted: 'Do I contradict myself? Yes I contradict myself. I am large. I contain multitudes.' Another and very different kind of American had held a similar opinion. Consistency, Emerson wrote, is 'the hobgoblin of little minds, adored by little statesmen and philosophers and divines. With consistency a great soul has simply nothing to do.' Maugham would never have thought of himself as 'a great soul'. But in his reflections about his life and his work, as in his creations of character on the stage and in print, he was indeed a multitudinous man.

'The Jester', by Sir Gerald Kelly (The Tate Gallery, London)

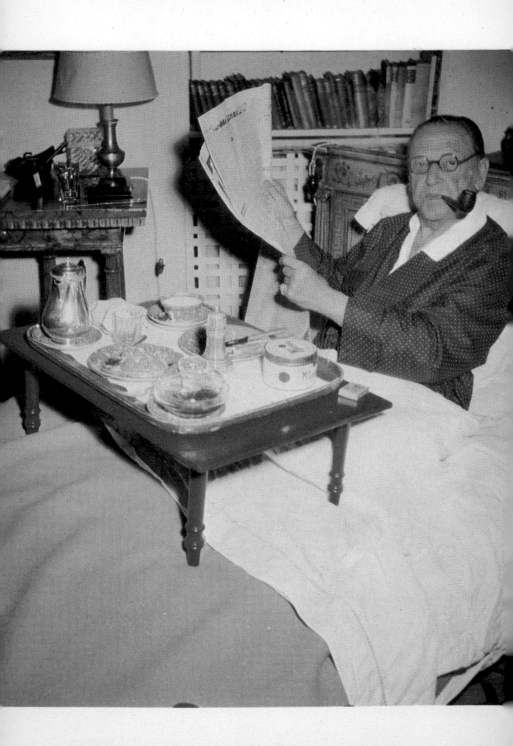

V. The Man

Somerset Maugham in 1946 (Radio Times Hulton Picture Library)

The later photographs of Maugham and the famous portrait by Graham Sutherland are pictures of misery. There is a look of twisted metal beneath a parchment skin. One can glimpse behind the strained, almost agonized features, the man who was concealing his distress by releasing a mordant wit. But what had become of the other self—the diner-out, the treasured guest of fashionable hostesses, the provider of excellent company, the man who said that he could never remember 'a good story' for conversational use but could be trusted, despite the hesitant speech, to cap another anecdote with the neat and memorable comment? What had become too of the all-conquering playwright of 1907 and subsequent years, the novelist always in demand?

Those must have been years spent 'on the top of happy hours' as Shakespeare, another middle-class arrival in fashionable society, wrote of his own emergence into august patronage and popular applause. It is impossible to think of the author as miserable after his release from poverty and doubts about his career. He could move from the best hotel in one capital to the next and voyage from one ocean to another sampling the islands of the aromatic East. Did he always wear the look of a harassed, even a tortured man? He said that he was never really happy in England and he was not obliged to stay there. There were sufficient reasons for a smile.

For men of his profession, as a mind as alert as his was bound to realize, there are certain to be slips from the summits into the crevasse of occasional and disconcerting failure. He naturally knew of the spites, jealousies and denigrations to which the trade of a writer is exposed. He was not innocent himself of these offences. He had put gall into the baking and brewing of *Cakes and Ale*.

Artists and authors, being in theory the devotees of the true, the beautiful, and the good should live, one may reasonably think, on a higher level of behaviour than the business men whom some arrogantly regard as 'clods without a spark'. Yet their world is rank with the weeds of acrimony and resentment. Death may urge sentimental journeys to funerals. Dickens wept at Thackeray's grave-side at Kensal Green. But, while the fight is on for reputations and rewards, the gloves are off. There is probably more friendship to be found amid the 'gin and Jaguars' of the stockbroker belt than among the coteries of Chelsea and the chattering absorbers of tepid cocktails in the salons of the lion-hunting hostesses at a get-together of the arriving authors and the 'booksy ladies'. Maugham did not regard riches as a proof of boorishness, but he had no taste for the roundabout of 'literary circles'. He could escape and did.

So why be wretched? Viewing money as a civilizing, not a demoralizing, asset, he had what he wanted and his defeats in the theatre were far less than his accumulation of success both there and in the book-shops, the libraries, and the editorial offices of the profitable magazines. He did not as a rule seem morose in company; on the few occasions when I met him in London he was sufficiently genial. He was not using his tongue as a stiletto, though one had been told that he could stab if he chose. But there is no doubt that when alone, he had more than his fair share of 'the dumps'. The description of his last years given by his nephew Robin in *Somerset and all the Maughams* presents a senility without sunshine, although the skies and seas were blue enough around the Villa Mauresque. The veteran with his tactful and patient secretary

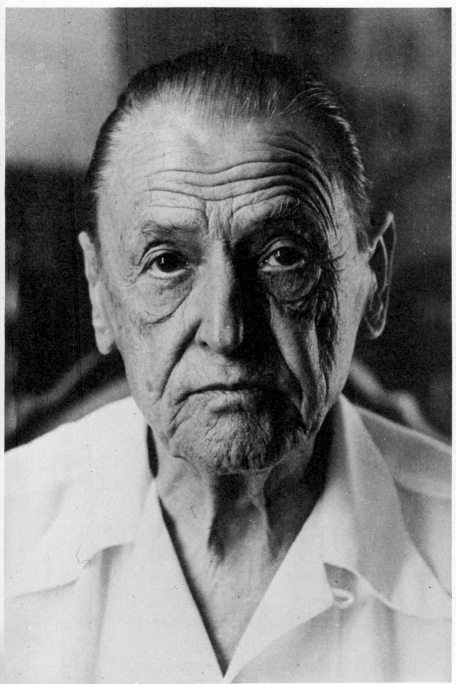

Somerset Maugham at Villa Mauresque, 1954 *(Syndication International)*

Villa Mauresque, 1954 *(Syndication International)*

Alan Searle, and attended by his ample and expert domestic staff had all the material comforts which he valued; yet he lacked tranquillity. In the shadows of the years he was given to self-accusation, broodings over a life that had gone wrong, misanthropic moods and splenetic outbursts.

The reasons for the despondency, which became more grievous with time, were several. Maugham could not shake off the orphan boy's sense of deprivation. Until the end, the photograph of his handsome mother was on the table beside his bed. She died eighty-seven years before he had his last look at the beloved face. In *The Summing Up* he related that 'When I was a small boy and unhappy, I used to dream night after night that my life at school was all a dream and that I should wake to find myself at home with my mother.' The wound, he said, was never healed.

The German wife of his far from sympathetic uncle and guardian at Whitstable had become almost a step-mother. She was kind and he wrote kindly of her. He might have resented her position as a substitute for the maternal ideal, but he was grateful for her simple goodness of heart. Yet the childhood memory remained and he was always in his way a haunted man whose fits of cynicism were in part the reactions of a frustrated tenderness of heart. He had his sentimental core. Had he been basically and completely tough, the scar, which he said was permanent, would have faded out of mind.

He was also afflicted by the lack of what is called 'a presence'. He was small and physically insignificant. If he was not known and welcomed as a notable, he could have entered company with little notice paid. He had a firm and prominent chin, usually regarded as a sign of pertinacity and rightly so in his case. To be small in stature is often to be stirred by vast ambition. Many of the world's conquerors, fighting their way to various kinds of leadership and power, have thrust the harder to reach the peaks of fame and power since they began some inches lower than their rivals. The handicapped and crippled can be very combative types. But they can retain a grievance about their lack of size, and Maugham would have been a less unhappy man if he had looked more impressive.

It is reasonable to wonder whether his antipathy to Hugh Walpole was not partly caused by the latter's imposing presence. Hugh in his time, was large, rubicund, seemingly aglow with health, noticeable anywhere, and obviously a Public Figure when

Somerset Maugham, with the final draft of his book of essays Ten Novelists and their Novels *in the rooftop 'den' at Villa Mauresque* (Syndication International)

Somerset Maugham discussing the next day's menus with his cook Annette (Syndication International)

Somerset Maugham and Alan Searle dining in the patio of Villa Mauresque (Syndication International)

he stood on the lecturer's dais where he performed so well and enjoyed himself so much. Walpole's speechifying came with an easy and persuasive flow. Maugham's stammer could be overcome on occasions. After his escape from France in 1940, he accepted an invitation from the B.B.C. to give a broadcast. The producer was nervous. Might not the distinguished guest find himself struggling with his words? There was no need for apprehension. With his text before him, his delivery was unimpeded. Yet to the end, he would hesitate at times in his conversation. Some of the remarks recorded by his nephew seem to gain by the fight for the word and the break in the sentence, but the fear of a sudden stop continued to be another of the scars.

Then there was the active dislike and even concealed contempt to which Willie was exposed by his elder brother Frederic. It is true Willie could hold his own in exchange of the uncomplimentary remark, but he smarted under the professional advancement and derisory attitude of the man who had all the qualities which the average Englishman admires. As schoolboy and undergraduate, Frederic was finely equipped to be a favourite. Willie was never good at games in which prowess meant popularity. Philip Carey, limping instead of stuttering through the early chapters of *Of Human Bondage*, presents a poignant picture of the sensitive lad among the louts of his own age and the third-rate pedagogues of Canterbury as he found them then. Frederic at Dover College had been Head Prefect and a prominent member of the football and cricket teams.

Then he went on to Trinity Hall at Cambridge where life was happy and glorious. He rowed for the University and was described in the university magazine as 'one of the best specimens of the all-round man that Cambridge can show at the present time. . . . He is a universal favourite in spite of his universal success.' To follow the legal profession was the Maugham tradition. Frederic made his way to the Bar and had some hard and impoverished years of waiting for briefs. (A barrister's career then did not advance so rapidly as it often does now.) He persevered and rose to the top. For an able barrister with political ambitions there were big rewards. He entered Parliament and was Lord Chancellor in Neville Chamberlain's Conservative Government at the time of Munich and the outbreak of the war. It seems that he did not preside tactfully over the Lords, but he had won the supreme prize.

Robin's memories of his triumphant father are not flattering.

Lord Maugham did not conceal the fact that he disliked and despised the no less successful Willie. What, he thought, was this business of telling stories and writing amusing plays? A Maugham should be above that kind of thing. It led to the keeping of bad company. Willie's friends were thought appalling and his extravagance shocking. He should have continued in the honourable profession of medicine. To Frederic an author of fiction—and fiction about such people as Willie chose for his subjects—was not a respectable member of the family.

This haughty detachment was not a silliness to be shrugged off by the younger man whose success in the theatre at the age of thirty-three had evoked a full-page cartoon in *Punch* in which Shakespeare stood looking baffled and gloomy beside the massed posters announcing four plays by W. Somerset Maugham running simultaneously in the chief London theatres. The brothers met. Frederic once stayed with Willie in the South of France. The latter's comment to Robin was, 'Your sainted father deigned to spend fourteen days beneath this roof without passing one single civil remark.' When Frederic was writing his autobiography at the great length of nearly a quarter of a million words, he asked Robin for a brief description of 'your three sisters and yourself and my brother Willie *in that order*'. For the five of them the limit of length was to be four lines! What finally was printed about the author-dramatist was this: 'I need not describe the works of my brother, William Somerset Maugham.' The relationship of the two remained embittered and their meeting in the Riviera sunshine did not thaw the ice. The better the days, the worse the tempers. The few frigid lines in Frederic's tome were typical of his desire and power to infuriate. He thought his brother's books disgusting and his way of life deplorable.

That Willie had homosexual inclinations was another cause of distress. It must be remembered that when he was twenty-two the trial and imprisonment of Oscar Wilde was a horrible event for those with tendencies which were then deemed unnatural and abominable and are now taken for granted in our permissive times. If Maugham had been wholly what is now called 'a queer', he would have had to be very careful, but there would have been a simplification of his life. He would not have entered on a marriage which was bound to be a failure.

His wife was Syrie Wellcome, whose first marriage, to Sir Henry Wellcome, was dissolved. She was good-looking and viva-

W. Somerset Maugham and Frederic Herbert Maugham in Bad Gastein, 1936, from a photograph by Lady Juliet Duff (Robin Maugham)

cious. Maugham was attracted by pretty women and it is noticeable that in his stories and plays there is abundance of ordinary love-making in and out of wedlock. Reading Maugham's fiction gives no impression that the author was in fact abnormal. He and Syrie would have been incompatible even if she had not discovered that one of his men friends meant more to him than she did.

That was Gerald Haxton, an unbiddable American. He was a heavy drinker and when 'high' he was irresponsible and reckless. He was once charged with gross indecency; though acquitted in court, he was later declared an undesirable alien and forbidden by the police to enter England. Inevitably Haxton's influence, fatal to marriage, was another cause of Frederic's indignation. It can be said on Haxton's behalf that he was a useful companion when Maugham was on his distant and sometimes dangerous travels; but few liked him and some loathed him. The friendship was a social folly and made it plain in an ugly way that Maugham was not a marriageable man. Robin reported his uncle's admission that his greatest mistake was the effort to persuade himself that he had ordinary habits. 'My greatest mistake,' he said, 'was that I tried to persuade myself that I was three-quarters normal and that only a quarter of me was queer, whereas it was really the other way round.' The melancholy mask in the portraits and photographs is the mark of that confusion.

'Disturbed' is now a favourite adjective of those making excuses for people who have got into trouble with the law. If the malefactors or unfortunates, according to the various views of crime and its causes, appear to have 'gone round the bend' they are spoken of as 'mentally disturbed'. There was a little clouding of Maugham's brain when he was over ninety and much given to self-reproach. Until the end his mind had been exceptionally acute and his writing a model of lucidity. But emotional disturbance had been there since boyhood. He could not overcome his early shyness and diffidence. He wanted to be popular and he missed the affection for which he craved. There was a daughter of his muddled marriage but he was not a family man. He strove to seem as other men, and he could manage that in company, but his inner life, never serene, became almost chaotic at its close. There were black hours during which he was more distraught than merely 'disturbed'.

He commended the resolution of those who committed suicide instead of prolonging an existence which had lost the essential values of life. He wished, he said, to die in his sleep, but he did

Syrie Maugham (centre) photographed at a party given by Victor Stiebel in Paris 1933
(Radio Times Hulton Picture Library)

not take the overdose of soporific pills which he could so easily have done. Instead, even when he was railing against the world and the frustrations of senility, he arranged to take one of the treatments which are claimed to assist longevity. It kept him physically preserved but it was a folly since it could only prolong the malaise of the mind.

His principal enjoyment had been work; after that came conversation and a game of bridge in both of which diversions he could hold his own with the best. There is occasional mention of golf and lawn tennis in his stories, but on the whole the familiar sports of his nation and his class did not interest him. One cannot visualize him as happy in the pavilion at Lords' cricket ground or in the grandstand at a football match. Watching human nature was his hobby, serving both as a recreation and a discovery of raw material.

In his handling of money there were absurd contrasts of the lavish and the parsimonious. His nephew described his insistence on travelling by bus in New York on a wintry day when he was a millionaire of seventy and had an appointment with his doctor. A taxi, he intimated brusquely, would be an absurd extravagance. Yet he made generous donations to his old school at Canterbury which he had hated. He provided hard tennis-courts, a boathouse, new science laboratories which cost ten thousand pounds and a library to which he also gave many books and some of his manuscripts for which American universities would now pay large sums. He remembered his fellow authors through generous gifts to the Authors' Society for young writers under thirty-five and a Travelling Scholarship with no restriction of age. The Royal Literary Fund for the relief of needy writers will also benefit largely in time from his will. Surely as a specialist in observing and recording oddities of character he must have smiled at himself when he would not pay a few shillings for a taxi.

Critical estimation rose at last. He was made a Companion of Honour in 1954. The more exalted Order of Merit had been given to John Galsworthy. Both men refused a knighthood which Maugham said had been offered him much earlier. He gave as his reason one with which Galsworthy would no doubt have sympathized. He thought that it would make him look ridiculous if, at a literary gathering, he was announced as Sir Somerset along with Mr Bennett, Mr Wells and Mr Shaw.

He knew that he had made mistakes as well as a fortune. He

Gerald Haxton, from a photograph taken in Paris 1934 (Robin Maugham)

could not guess how many readers he would continue to have in his absence. For his plays he expected little or no future, since he regarded theatrical success as essentially dated and transient. Because he belonged to no coterie and wrote for no coterie his acceptance in the future by a huge public and the acquisition of new readers are more than probable. All his best books are available in paper-back editions at popular prices and were continually being reprinted in the nineteen-sixties. Despite some periods of bad health he achieved longevity. Brief life will not be the fate of his work. The ennobled Frederic has been forgotten. Willie's name endures.

Somerset Maugham on the terrace of Villa Mauresque (Syndication International)

Summary of Events

1874: Born in Paris

1882: Attends French School for children in Paris
Death of his mother

1884: Death of his father. The orphan is sent to live with his uncle, the Rev. Henry Macdonald Maugham, at his vicarage in Whitstable

1884: Goes to King's School, Canterbury

1889: Leaves King's School, Canterbury

1891: Student at Heidelberg University

1892: Entered St. Thomas's Hospital in London as a medical student

1897: Qualified as a doctor. His first novel is published

1898: Goes into lodgings in London and begins to be busy as a writer. Small success for some years
Travels in Spain

1904: In Paris

1908: Triumphant break-through as a dramatist with four plays running in the West End

1914: Works as doctor at the Front in France and Belgium.

1915: Transferred to Secret Service. Spying on spies in Switzerland provides material for 'Ashenden' stories

1916: Married to Syrie, divorced wife of Sir Henry Wellcome
Goes to New York, crosses U.S.A., and begins his voyages among the islands in the Pacific

1917: Ordered to Russia on secret service. Crosses by train from Vladivostock to Petrograd.
After inevitable failure of his mission and collapse of Kerensky's unstable Government he escapes to Sweden and thence to Britain with broken health

1918: Treated successfully for tuberculosis in Scotland

1919: In U.S.A.

1922: Extensive travel in Malaya, Borneo and the Pacific Islands

1923: In Burma. The dispersed travel continues

1933: In Spain

1936: In West Indies

1938: In India

1940: Escapes to Bordeaux from his home in South of France and crosses to U.S.A.

1946: Returns to England and determines to leave it.
Settles in South of France

1954: Made a Companion of Honour

1961: Presents Maugham Library to King's School, Canterbury

1965: Dies, December 16

Books

Liza of Lambeth, novel, 1897
Orientations, short stories, 1899
The Hero, novel, 1901
Mrs. Craddock, novel, 1902
The Land of the Blessed Virgin, travel, 1905
The Bishop's Apron, novel, 1906
The Explorer, novel, 1907
The Magician, novel, 1908
Of Human Bondage, novel, 1915
The Moon and Sixpence, novel, 1919
The Trembling of a Leaf, short stories, 1921
On a Chinese Screen, travel, 1922
The Painted Veil, novel, 1925
The Casuarina Tree, short stories, 1926
Ashenden, short stories, 1928
The Gentleman in the Parlour, travel, 1930
Cakes and Ale, novel, 1930
First Person Singular, short stories, 1931
The Narrow Corner, novel, 1932
Ah King, short stories, 1933
Altogether, short stories, 1934
Don Fernando, travel, 1935
Cosmopolitans, short stories, 1936
Theatre, novel, 1937
The Summing Up, reflections on life and work, 1938
Christmas Holiday, novel, 1939
The Mixture as Before, short stories, 1940
France at War, general, 1940
Books and You, general, 1940
Up at the Villa, novel, 1941
Strictly Personal, general, 1941
Then and Now, novel, 1946
Creatures of Circumstance, short stories, 1947
Catalina, novel, 1948
Quartet, four stories with film scripts, 1948
A Writer's Note-book, Memories and Thoughts, 1949
Trio, three stories with film scripts, 1950
The Complete Short Stories in three volumes, 1951
The Vagrant Mood, essays, 1952
Encore, three film scripts, 1952
Ten Novels and Their Authors, criticism, 1954
Points of View, essays, 1958
Purely for My Pleasure, about his pictures, with colour plates, 1962
Selected Prefaces and Introductions, criticism, 1964

Plays

The dates are those of the first productions (London or New York). In the case of a play not so presented the date is that of publication in book form.

A Man of Honour, 1904
Lady Frederick, 1907
The Explorer, 1908
Jack Straw, 1908
Mrs. Dot, 1908
Penelope, 1909
Smith, 1909
Grace, 1911
Landed Gentry, 1913
The Land of Promise, 1914
Caroline, 1916
Our Betters, 1917
Love in a Cottage, 1918
Home and Beauty, 1919
Caesar's Wife, 1919
The Unknown, 1920
The Circle, 1921
East of Suez, 1922
The Unattainable, 1923
The Camel's Back, 1924
Loaves and Fishes, 1924
The Letter, 1927
The Constant Wife, 1927
The Sacred Flame, 1928
The Breadwinner, 1930
For Services Rendered, 1932
Sheppey, 1933

A Select Bibliography

Aldington, Michael. *Somerset Maugham.*
Brophy, John. *Somerset Maugham.* British Council.
MacCarthy, S. Desmond. *Somerset Maugham.*
Maugham, Robin. *Somerset and All the Maughams.* Longman/Heinemann.
Ward, R. H. *Somerset Maugham.*